CANADIAN CULTURAL
NATIONALISM

The Canadian Institute of International Affairs and the Council on Foreign Relations co-sponsored the Fourth Lester B. Pearson Conference on the Canada-U.S. Relationship, on which this publication is based. All statements of fact and expressions of opinion contained in it, however, are the sole responsibility of the authors.

The Canadian Institute of International Affairs has as its objects the stimulation in Canada of more informed opinion on international affairs and more particularly on Canada's international role and interests, and the study of international affairs in its broadest sense with primary emphasis on the economic, political, social, diplomatic, and defence roles and interests of Canada.

The Council on Foreign Relations, Inc., is a non-profit and non-partisan organization devoted to promoting improved understanding of international affairs through the free exchange of ideas. Its membership of about 1,700 persons throughout the United States is made up of individuals with special interest and experience in international affairs. The Council has no affiliation with, and receives no funding from, the United States government. The Council does not take any position on questions of foreign policy.

CANADIAN CULTURAL NATIONALISM

The Fourth
Lester B. Pearson Conference
on the
Canada-United States Relationship

Janice L. Murray, Editor

Published for the

Canadian Institute of International Affairs

and the

Council on Foreign Relations

by

New York University Press: New York: 1977

Library of Congress Catalog Card Number: 77-015362
ISBN: 0-8147-5421-X

Manufactured in the United States of America

PREFACE

The following series of chapters on Canadian cultural nationalism and how the United States is affected by it are an informal report of a conference held in September 1976. Much
has happened since then that has affected and will continue
to have an impact on the topics discussed at the conference
and the papers written before and after it. The victory in
Quebec of the Parti Québécois -- to single out one highly
visible change -- occurred in November 1976 and qualifies
somewhat the remarks about Quebec in this volume. Despite
this and other developments, however, the individual essays
have been left in their original form. This book is not intended to be an exhaustive examination of the subject but
rather is an informal bringing together of material which the
conference organizers believe will interest people who did
not participate in the actual conference. Each chapter has
been dated and stands as a statement of the author's thoughts
and feelings at the time it was written.

In his introductory essay, "The Why and Wherefore,"
Robert W. Reford, Executive Director of the Canadian Institute
of International Affairs, discusses the history of the Pearson
conferences, the background of binational and global events
against which they were held, and the work of this fourth conference. In addition, introductory notes to Parts I and II
describe what each author was asked to do and the relation of
the essays to one another. Here it will suffice to comment
particularly on the binational character of the book. Because
Canadian and American authors contributed equally to the pro-
ject, and because it is the product of efforts in both countries, differences in Canadian and American spellings and
usage have been left intact.

The Pearson conferences were the result of efforts by a
number of individuals and organizations in Canada and the

United States. In his introduction, Robert Reford expresses
the gratitude to them of the two sponsoring organizations,
the Canadian Institute of International Affairs and the Council on Foreign Relations. Here it is particularly appropriate to echo his thanks to the Charles F. Kettering Foundation
for its support of this publication. Appreciation also is
due here to the individuals without whose unflagging interest
and efforts this book would not have been possible: Robert
Valkenier (Council editor), Marion Magee (Institute editor),
William Diebold, Jr. (Senior Research Fellow of the Council),
and Robert W. Reford. And, finally, it is impossible to thank
John Sloan Dickey adequately for his enthusiasm and guidance
throughout all the conferences and the making of this volume.

J.L.M.
September 1977

CONFERENCE PARTICIPANTS

Roland Michener, P.C., C.C., Conference Chairman
  Governor General of Canada, 1967-1974; President, Canadian
  Institute of International Affairs

John Sloan Dickey, Chairman, U.S. delegation
  President Emeritus, Dartmouth College

Robert W. Reford, Chairman, Canadian delegation
  Executive Director, Canadian Institute of International
  Affairs

Willis C. Armstrong
  Consultant to the United States Council and the International Chamber of Commerce

Michael Barkway, Canadian rapporteur
  Editor and Publisher of The Financial Times of Canada,
  1962-1974

Jacques J. Bernard
  Retired business executive; past President of the Winnipeg
  Builders Exchange

James Stacy Coles
  President, Research Corporation, New York

Ramsay Cook
  Professor of History, York University, Toronto

William Diebold, Jr.
  Senior Research Fellow, Council on Foreign Relations

Peter C. Dobell
  Director, Parliamentary Centre for Foreign Affairs and Foreign Trade, Ottawa

André Fortier
  Under Secretary of State, Government of Canada

Robert Fulford
  Editor, Saturday Night

Alfred O. Hero, Jr.
  Director and Secretary, World Peace Foundation

John W. Holmes
   Research Director, Canadian Institute of International
   Affairs

Janice L. Murray, U.S. rapporteur
   Assistant to the Director of Studies, Council on Foreign
   Relations

Richard H. Nolte
   Executive Director, Institute of Current World Affairs

Joseph S. Nye
   Professor of Government, Harvard University

Calvin G. Rand
   President, Niagara Institute for International Studies

James M. Read
   Consultant in International Affairs, Charles F. Kettering
   Foundation

G. S. Shortliffe
   Special Assistant, Department of External Affairs

Denis Smith
   Editor, Canadian Forum

Henry P. Smith III
   Chairman, U.S. Section, International Joint Commission

Rufus Z. Smith
   Executive Director of Visitor Program Service of Meridian
   House International

Roger Frank Swanson
   Acting Director and Associate Professor at the Center of
   Canadian Studies, Johns Hopkins School of Advanced Inter-
   national Studies

Bernard Trotter
   Head of Academic Planning, Queen's University

Richard D. Vine
   Deputy Assistant Secretary of State for Canadian Affairs

Dagmar Wichmar
   Programme Coordinator, Canadian Institute of Internationa
   Affairs

CONTENTS

1.

THE WHY AND WHEREFORE

Robert W. Reford

How fortunate we are to have such a great people as the Canadians to share the northern boundaries of our continent. . . .
On behalf of all of us, I extend to you our most sincere
gratitude for your unceasing co-operation and friendliness
toward us and may our two nations forever set an example for
the rest of the world, showing how two countries can live
side by side in peace and harmony.
          --Glenn S. Banner, Lancaster, Pa., Letter to the
              editor, The Toronto Star, December 8, 1976.

As we witness the transition of power to a new administration
in Washington, we realize how relatively unimportant are the
issues of Canadian-American relations. Our bilateral problems
are far down on the agenda, compared with the effort to control the spread of nuclear weapons, the search for peace in
Southern Africa and the Middle East, the intricate problems
of relations with the Third World, the consequences of a further increase in the price of oil, and the overwhelming global questions of pollution, population, and starvation. And
this list leaves domestic questions to one side.

    Yet, as Glenn Banner's letter indicates, relations be-
tween our two countries have a certain significance. They
are held up as a working model which others should try to
emulate, or as a concrete example of how the principles set
out in the Final Act of the Conference on Security and Co-operation in Europe (Helsinki, 1975) have operated in practice,
without any undue effort, over a considerable period of time.
Because the two nations are so interdependent in so many
areas, their relations can be subjected to stresses and
strains which might not become as apparent (or as abrasive)

- 1 -

between other neighbours; and because the relationship can be envied by others, it demands special care and attention.

It is against this broad background that the series of four Lester B. Pearson Conferences organized by the Canadian Institute of International Affairs and the Council on Foreign Relations between 1971 and 1976 has been held. As they have been designed to examine the relationship between Canada and the United States in the 1970s -- each conference emphasizing some particular aspect which has been causing or might be expected to cause concern -- a brief closer look at the last decade of Canadian-American relations is in order.

The first Pearson conference met in the shadow of President Nixon's emergency economic measures of August 15, 1971. These were a traumatic event for Canadians, who discovered that, far from being overlooked or forgotten, Canada was regarded by the U.S. Treasury Department as one of those responsible for the crisis. It might be flattering to be put in the same economic boat as the European Community and Japan, but Ottawa was disturbed by the way such nationalistic measures were introduced virtually without warning.

Canadians probably had forgotten that a year earlier their government had acted unilaterally by passing the Arctic Waters Pollution Prevention Act, which established a pollution control zone in waters north of 60 degrees and extending for 100 miles from the coast. Within this area, all ships would be required to conform to Canadian standards. In addition, the government extended the territorial sea to 12 miles and imposed fisheries closing lines across major bodies of water, including the Gulf of St. Lawrence and the seas east and south of the Queen Charlotte Islands. Furthermore, Canada announced a reservation to acceptance of the compulsory jurisdiction of the International Court of Justice. This action led to a strong protest from the United States.

In two years, each country had offended the other, though each could make a cogent argument to justify what it had done. It is nevertheless appropriate to ask whether this was symptomatic of a change in their relationship.

In retrospect, 1968 can be regarded as a turning point. In Canada, Pierre Elliott Trudeau became Prime Minister, and one of his first announcements was that there would be a major review of foreign policy. As a new man, he was anxious to move in new directions. In the United States, Richard Nixon was elected President. Although a veteran politician, he too was determined to break with the past. The two men, so different in their background and experience, were both inclined to stress domestic rather than international priorities, which gave their foreign policies a tinge of nationalism. This was popular with their electorates. The Canadian voter appeared more interested in seeing his country take an identifiable stand. Quiet diplomacy was no longer acceptable and had, in fact, come to be regarded as synonymous with following Washington's lead. Americans, for their part, were becoming increasingly restive under the responsibilities of international leadership, which they regarded as having to act as the world's policeman. Vietnam was typical of what was perceived to be a potential consequence, and by 1969 there was widespread disillusionment with the war.

While it may be true that Trudeau realized his new directions would have to include a readjustment of relations with Washington, there is no evidence that Canada figured in Nixon's thoughts (or those of his influential adviser Henry Kissinger). But change there would have to be. The Committee for an Independent Canada was formally established in 1970, and one of its most influential founders was Walter Gordon who, as Minister of Finance in the Pearson government, had pursued a policy designed to reduce Canadian economic dependence on the United States. The extent of this dependence rapidly became evident in the wake of the measures of August 15, which reportedly affected 3 per cent of Canada's GNP. It was estimated that between 40,000 and 100,000 Canadians might lose their jobs if the surcharge on U.S. imports remained in effect for a year. Small wonder, then, that Canadian ministers had immediately gone to Washington to seek an exemption, as they had done from the Interest Equalization Tax in 1963 and the mandatory regulations regarding direct capital investment in 1968. In 1971, this request was denied. The balance of trade was running in Canada's favour, and the American deficit had caused the crisis. The Treasury Department, regarding Canada as a contributing factor, called for an adjustment in Canada's trading position rather than an exemption from the emergency measures.

Clearly, this marked the end of a special relationship between the two countries, in the sense that special treatment might be involved. Inevitably, however, there would be a special quality to the relationship because the two countries shared a continent and had the largest total flow of bilateral trade in the world. But after August 15, this would be more a relationship of equality. After some initial hesitation, that relationship seemed to suit Trudeau's more independent approach. He did go to Washington in December 1971 "to seek reassurance from the President . . . that it is neither the intention nor the desire of the United States that the economy of Canada become so dependent on the United States in terms of a trading pattern that Canadians will inevitably lose independence of economic decision."[1] On his return, he was able to tell the House of Commons that Nixon had said "it was in the interests of the United States to have a Canadian neighbour which was independent both politically and economically"; Trudeau described this as "fantastic."

In October 1972, the Canadian government filled a gaping hole in its foreign policy review by publishing a paper on relations with the United States, under the title <u>Canada-U.S. Relations: Options for the Future</u>. It listed these three alternatives for policy directions:

> (a) we can seek to maintain more or less our present relationship with the United States with a minimum of policy adjustments;

> (b) we can move deliberately toward closer integration with the United States;

> (c) we can pursue a comprehensive, long-term strategy to develop and strengthen the Canadian economy and other aspects of our national life and in the process to reduce the present Canadian vulnerability.[2]

To no one's surprise, it rapidly became evident that the government supported the third option.

The Pearson conferences, therefore, have been held at a most appropriate time. It was a period of change in the attitude of the two governments, inspired to a degree by a change in personalities but more fundamentally by changed circumstances. It was also a period of ferment in the issues which confronted the foreign offices of the world. No longer was it possible to think of foreign policy in terms of relations between countries. The questions were of quite a different nature: pollution, population, inflation, starvation. The concern was with energy and resources, with economic development and human rights. These cut across established lines, involving several departments of government, indeed different levels of government.

In addition, there were the beginnings of change in public attitudes in North America, especially in the United

States. It had been a long-time complaint of Canadians that they knew more about the United States than Americans knew about Canada, and there was a good deal of foundation for this apart from the stories of tourists arriving in July with skis on the car. In the 1970s, things started to be different, and Canadians were not always happy as a result. They found that their country was seen as a haven for draft-dodgers; as a supporter of Communist China and Cuba by its insistence on trading with those two countries and being on speaking terms with them; as a place which seemed to be selfish in hoarding its energy supplies and refusing to part with its surplus of clean water; and as a country possibly on the way to dissolution as the result of separatism in Quebec. Canadians might look back nostalgically to the days when they were treated with benign neglect.

The concept of the Pearson conferences arose from the appointment of John Sloan Dickey as the Whitney H. Shepardson Senior Visiting Fellow at the Council on Foreign Relations for 1971-72 with the intention of examining the U.S. interest in an independent Canada. As one of the early preparatory steps in his work, which resulted in his book, Canada and the American Presence, he consulted John W. Holmes, then Director-General of the Canadian Institute of International Affairs, and they agreed to organize a select conference of not more than fifteen persons from each country to discuss the relationship. This meeting was held in October 1971, and prominent among the participants was the Rt. Hon. Lester B. Pearson, the former Prime Minister of Canada, in whose honour the conferences were named after his death in 1972.

The conferences have been private. The purpose was not to work out agreed solutions, nor to make policy. Rather, it was to gain deeper understanding through informed discussion, and it was hoped that those present would share this experience with others. The conference reports have been designed for circulation to participants, and speakers have not been identified by name. This approach is in the tradition of both the Council and the Institute, and its objective is to enable everyone to speak freely. Both organizations have made a point of including representatives from the appropriate government departments and agencies to ensure that the views and experiences of those charged with implementing policy were presented; but they were invited personally and not as official representatives. It has proved harder to involve elected politicians, largely because they have been reluctant to spare the amount of time involved. Delegations have included experts from the business and academic worlds, as well as people with a more general knowledge of the particular issue but with a special interest in relations between the two countries. The mix of policy-makers and academic critics, of representatives from the public and private sectors, of generalists and specialists has proved successful and stimulating.

If it appears from what follows that undue attention has been paid to Canadian concerns, this can be explained by the natural feeling of a smaller partner that it may be taken for granted, or that it may be trampled underfoot in an absent-minded moment. As Prime Minister Trudeau has said, "Living next to you [Americans] is in some ways like sleeping with an elephant: No matter how friendly and even-tempered is the beast, one is affected by every twitch and grunt."[3]

The agenda for the first conference put the basic question to be considered as follows: What should the two countries want: bilaterally, multilaterally? It then listed these four main topics: a concept for the relationship; problem-solving in the relationship; national attitudes and the perception of each other by the two countries; the American stake in an independent Canada.

Taking a look backward from the perspective of five years, Dickey has said that no one would have written that kind of agenda in 1976. It was, in a sense, too introspective, too mechanistic, and too concerned with concepts and procedures.

The starting point for the agenda was the Heeney-Merchant report, submitted in 1965 by two men who had each served two terms as his country's ambassador to the other nation. Their study had been undertaken at the request of President Lyndon Johnson and Prime Minister Pearson, and it was titled <u>Principles of Partnership</u>. The first Pearson conference confirmed what had already become apparent, namely, that however admirable its basic premise might have been, the report marked the end rather than the beginning of an era. The phrase "partnership" was no longer acceptable as a description of the relationship, and a rising tide of Canadian nationalism was becoming evident. The participants at that conference agreed that the relationship was facing a crisis, but no consensus emerged either within or between the two delegations on how it could be tackled. They did agree it could not be left untended, and this led the sponsoring organizations to decide that further conferences should follow, each focussing on a single issue or a cluster of related issues.

The twin topics of energy and continental defence were selected for the second Pearson conference, which was held April 25-28, 1973. Continental defence was expected to be timely because the NORAD agreement was up for renewal in May. However, it almost turned out to be a non-topic because of the announcement on the eve of the conference of the Canadian government's decision to renew. Yet the exchange of views was sufficiently disturbing to one participant that he studied the defence relationship between the two countries in depth because he was afraid the two governments were talking past, rather than to, each other.

It was energy which really brought the discussion to life. Certainly, with the advantage of hindsight, one can say it was a prophetic occasion. The consequences of a growing United States dependence on imports, especially from the Middle East, were outlined. There seemed to be a consensus that the energy message which the President had recently sent to Congress was not strong enough, perhaps because he shrank from imposing stern measures when the average American was not aware of a crisis. Six months later came the Yom Kippur War, the Arab oil boycott, and a crisis which affected everyone. There were fascinating insights into the energy business: how the first explorations for oil on the North Slope of Alaska began in 1949, but oil was not discovered until 1967, and it probably would not be on stream before 1978; how the actual discovery came when the company concerned had virtually given up hope, only continuing to drill because it was cheaper than dismantling the rig and shipping it out; of the efforts made to meet the objections of the environmental groups, many of whom refused to be convinced because they did not want to see the American way of life perpetuated.

I remember my personal sense of shock when someone spoke of war. Traditionally, he said, a nation deprived of a vital resource had been prepared to fight for it. Oil was such a resource, and there was no reason to believe that a nation whose supplies were cut off would not fight. Mercifully, his prophecy has not been fulfilled; but it was, as the Duke of Wellington said of the Battle of Waterloo, a damned close thing.

The view was expressed that Canada was better off than the United States because it was virtually self-sufficient in energy, but the question was asked: What happens if Windsor, Ontario, is warm and Detroit is cold? Can Canada afford to refuse exports simply to meet its own demands? Should it not be neighbourly enough to share shortages? (In 1977, with record cold waves in the Northeast, Canada authorized additional exports of natural gas.)

Looking back, one can say that the world energy crisis developed more rapidly than even the pessimists at that second conference had anticipated, reaching its climax in a matter of months rather than years. Equally, Canada's complacency about being self-sufficient, at least for hydrocarbons, turned out to be an illusion. By 1975, the government had been forced to announce that its estimates of reserves had proved optimistic and that it would have to phase out all oil exports to the United States. This did not provoke a major crisis, largely because there was excellent consultation and the exports have been reduced gradually rather than cut off in one step.

It was the discussion on defence which opened up part of the topic for the third conference held in September 1974: multinational corporations, international unionism, and Canadian industrial strategy. Continuation of the defence-production-sharing arrangements between Canada and the United States brought on a spirited exchange. Canada had built up a substantial surplus as a result of the Vietnam War, and Washington was pressing for an adjustment as part of its follow-up to the August 15 emergency. A Canadian rejected the need for change, saying that maintenance of the defence-production programme was an essential part of Canada's industrial strategy. An American replied there was no way the U.S. government could accept such an argument as decisive.

Canada's industrial strategy thus emerged as a possible friction point. It was also a subject of controversy among Canadians. Tied in with it were employment policies, the regulation of foreign investment, regional development, and, of course, trade policy. Americans were concerned that industrial strategy would lead to new trade barriers while in their own country the Burke-Hartke bill reflected pressure not only for protectionism but also for control over foreign investments. But the American labour unions, who were the strongest backers of the bill as a way of preventing what they thought was the "export of jobs," had many affiliates in Canada. How could they serve the interests of all their members? In Canada, international unionism was itself being challenged by growing nationalism. At the same time, many people saw international union action as the natural defence of labour's interests against the multinational corporation.

As the labour issue was the least familiar, it was decided that the conference should focus on these matters but relate them to industrial strategy and the multinational corporation. This decision resulted in some fascinating debate, but in retrospect it was the least satisfying of the four Pearson conferences. That is a subjective judgment which needs to be qualified. By usual standards, it was a successful conference; but to those who had experienced the stimulation of Pearson I and the almost electrifying excitement of Pearson II, it was a let-down.

Why was this so? Had we bitten off more than we could chew and created an indigestible lump of topics? Had we failed to go far enough to establish the relevance of the topics to one another? As the organizers planned the agenda, they believed they had found some intriguing issues in the links connecting multinationals, international unions, and industrial strategy; but at the conference these were never fully picked up and explored. Part of the problem was that, as a result of an unfortunate combination of circumstances, a number of labour union officials were at the last minute kept from attending. Some who were there challenged the premises of the agenda. The autonomy of Canadian components of the international unions was increasingly recognized, it was said. From the point of view of some American unionists, there is "a Negro problem, a Chicano problem, a woman problem, but no Canadian problem." It was not altogether clear whether this degree of harmony resulted from a keen appreciation of the benefits of international unionism, a solution of past problems, or the tendency to ignore them -- as suggested by the accusation that whatever individual unions did, the AFL-CIO as an organization was quite unaware of Canada.

The topic for the fourth Pearson conference was Canadian cultural nationalism, and it took place September 22-25, 1976. Its deliberations are the subject of this volume. While the second and third conferences had attempted to link several issues, this time a single theme was selected. It was, however, one which embraced a variety of subtopics: magazines, radio, and television (both in terms of ownership and content); book publishing; education, especially American professors at Canadian universities; stage and screen actors and directors; even sports. Superimposed was a deliberate attempt to examine the different attitudes of Quebec and the rest of the country. It was recalled that Pearson himself had expressed at the first conference his view that cultural questions would probably become a major difficulty between the two countries. In contrast, the Options for the Future paper of October 1972 almost dismissed this possibility. "It is one of the areas in which Canadians can act with the least risk of external repercussion," it said. This has proved over-optimistic.

Canadian cultural nationalism is as old as Canada. It is also, as Dickey has written, "inescapably (and that is precisely the right word) a reaction to the American presence, past and current."[4] If it is likely to be with us for a long time to come, there is good reason to examine it in more detail. The papers prepared for the fourth Pearson conference provide an excellent introduction to its history, to French Canadian nationalism, and to how the American public interest may be affected. There is also some value in an account of how this issue was perceived by a group of interested Americans and Canadians meeting on the eve of the election of Jimmy Carter to the presidency and of René Lévesque to be Premier of Quebec.

Before letting the participants speak for themselves, a word of appreciation must be expressed to the Niagara Institute. The first Pearson conference was its inaugural event, and the sponsoring organizations were more than happy to hold the subsequent meetings there. It is difficult to imagine a more congenial host. The Niagara Institute was created by Calvin Rand, and the meetings have been held in Randwood, his family estate at Niagara-on-the-Lake. The Rand family still use it, and the conferees are literally guests for the occasion. The opportunity to meet in a historic house which is still very much lived in has helped create the atmosphere of friendliness, comradeship, and informality that has been such a feature of the Pearson conferences. Of course, acting as host for such occasions is only one of the purposes of the Niagara Institute, whose other activities are a story in themselves.

Finally, a word of thanks must be expressed to the Charles F. Kettering Foundation for its generous support to the Council on Foreign Relations, which made the series possible, and for its encouragement of and great interest in all phases of the conferences. We are also most grateful to the Foundation for its enthusiasm for and support of this publication. In addition, a grant by the Donner Foundation enabled the Council to step up its Canadian activities and supported John Dickey's fellowship in particular. For its part, the Canadian Institute of International Affairs is most grateful to the Ford Foundation for its support of the first conference; to the J. W. Dafoe Foundation for its support of the second and third conferences; and, for the fourth conference, to supporters who wish to remain anonymous. Our appreciation is more than perfunctory. All who bave attended a Pearson conference have left with an indelible memory of the occasion. The conferences have been informative, provocative, stimulating, and perhaps most important, enjoyable.

January 1977

NOTES

1. House of Commons, Debates, December 7, 1971, p. 10205.

2. International Perspectives, Special Issue, Autumn 1972, p. 13.

3. Pierre Elliott Trudeau, Address to the National Press Club, Washington, D.C., March 25, 1969.

4. John Sloan Dickey, Canada and the American Presence: The United States Interest in an Independent Canada (New York: New York University Press, for the Council on Foreign Relations, 1975), p. xi.

PART I

DEFINING ISSUES

Some Discussion Papers

Several background papers were written for the benefit of
the conference participants. Three of them are included
here. Since very few Americans have any knowledge of the
wellsprings and evolution of Canadian cultural nationalism,
one of the most important needs for the majority of American
participants was an explanation of the historical foundation
of the issues that would be discussed at the conference. Accordingly, the first paper, written by Ramsay Cook, Professor
of History at York University (Toronto), is an interpretation of the developments leading to contemporary Canadian
concerns and actions.

Quebec holds a special place in any consideration of
Canadian culture, of Canadian nationalism, or of the two
combined. In the second paper, Solange Chaput Rolland, a
Quebec journalist, gives a highly personal statement of the
meaning of cultural nationalism to a Québécoise, discussing
the relationship of Quebec to anglophone Canada and to
France, and of politics and economics to culture.

These papers, which confront issues of cultural nationalism from Canadian perspectives, also raise the question: What is the nature of the U.S. interest in Canada's
thinking and action about these issues? Although the conference focused on Canada, American reactions and certain
elements of U.S. policy were involved. For instance, the
Canadian government decision to cease granting tax deductions to Canadian businesses for their advertising in the
Canadian edition of Time magazine clearly affected a private
American interest. This and other examples demonstrated

that some private American interests are harmed by Canadian actions inspired by cultural nationalism. A second, related question then arises: Does the United States have a national public interest in Canadian cultural nationalism, either because of the effects on private interests or for broader reasons? In the third paper, Roger Frank Swanson, Associate Professor and Acting Director of the Center of Canadian Studies at the Johns Hopkins University School of Advanced International Studies, examines these related issues.

2.

CULTURAL NATIONALISM IN CANADA:
AN HISTORICAL PERSPECTIVE

Ramsay Cook

Have we survived?
If so, what happens _after_ Survival?
       --Margaret Atwood, _Survival_.

What in heaven's name do we have to do in Canada to prove to
the world that we are not hick nationalists? We are in the
vanguard of internationalism and have been for some time. . . .
We stand next to no one in the wholesale abandonment of a national culture and far from lamenting the loss, no one even
waved good-bye because we were so busy saying hello to its re-
placement. . . . Canada in the throes of nationalism? Don't
make me laugh. It is in the throes of nothing. As usual.
       --John Fraser, _The Globe and Mail_, June 19, 1976.

Continentalism is treason.
       --S. M. Crean, _Who's Afraid of Canadian Culture?_

"The very word Americanization is a challenge to us; for though
we are Canadians, we also live in America," a leading Canadian
novelist remarked in 1929. "Are we going to allow ourselves
to be identified with that tendency of our neighbours to the
south which bids fair to recast the established values of life?
The fight is on between the ancient ideals of Europe and those
of this new America which is asserting itself from day to day."[1]
Frederick Philip Grove expressed here a dilemma which has never
ceased to puzzle both Canadians and foreigners who have attempted
to make sense of Canadian culture. What values should characterize Canadian life: those inherited from Europe, or those developed in response to North American conditions? And would either
of these alternatives assure the growth of an indigenous Canadian
culture, one dominated neither by the standards of Europe nor by
those of the United States?

In the almost unending discussion of this dilemma the meaning of the word "culture" has never been entirely clear. Not surprisingly perhaps, for, as Raymond Williams has recently observed, culture "is one of the two or three most complicated words in the English language."[2] For some it has quite obviously meant "high culture": music, art, literature, and philosophy. But more frequently it has meant something broader, vaguer, and more emotional: a set of social values or a way of life. That second sense of culture is the one intended by nationalists, at least since Herder at the end of the eighteenth century developed the idea of separate cultures, rather than one culture or civilization.

In contemporary Canada there can be no doubt that cultural nationalists, whether discussing education, broadcasting, painting, or literature, are using the term "culture" in a very broad sense. Evidence of this contention is at hand. Margaret Atwood's Survival, though presented as a thematic guide to Canadian literature, is in fact a quest for the meaning of the entire Canadian experience.[3] In that she is following in a track set out by many Canadian historians over several generations.[4] The ongoing debate about foreign professors in Canadian universities, or about the impact of American social science methodology, has always been couched in terms of Canadian values as contrasted with "internationalist" or "imperialist" values.[5] A similar anxiety runs through a recent socio-economic study of the corporate structure of the Canadian economy,[6] as it does in a rather clumsy nationalist-Marxist attempt to reinterpret the history of Canadian art.[7] Even some Canadian writers on sport, especially the national sport of hockey, discuss their subject in the context of a Canadian culture. ("If we cannot save hockey we cannot save Canada," Bruce Kidd and John Macfarlane claim dramatically.[8]) Finally, and in a somewhat confused fashion, a new book entitled Who's Afraid of Canadian Culture?, while focusing upon cultural institutions, is preoccupied with the value system, the way of life, that those institutions allegedly fail to reflect and sustain.[9]

The fact is, then, that Canadian cultural nationalists are rarely concerned with simple or specific questions such as the percentage of foreign curators of art galleries in Canada, the amount of advertising revenue scooped up by the Canadian edition of Reader's Digest, or the volume of American-produced cable TV that is beamed into Canada. These things are merely symbols of what is more basic: the challenge of Americanization. Or, in a more positive sense, Canadian cultural nationalists want to preserve, or develop, a set of social or cultural values that will guarantee Canadian distinctiveness from

the United States. Once that is understood, it is not difficult to comprehend the cultural nationalist's conviction that
state intervention, direction, and even ownership must be
seen as fundamental to the whole process of differentiating
Canada from the United States. It is not merely that the state
alone has the resources necessary to finance cultural survival,
though that is important; it is also that a statist or socialist approach to culture would in itself be evidence that Canadian culture is different from the free enterprise culture of
the United States. Though expressed more frequently in recent
years than in the past, this view is hardly a new one. Indeed,
its clearest expression came as early as 1932 when Graham Spry,
a leading supporter of a publicly owned broadcasting system in
Canada, told a parliamentary committee that:

> Why are the American interests so interested in the
> Canadian situation? The reason is clear. In the
> first place, the American chains have regarded Canada
> as part of their field and consider Canada as in a
> state of radio tutelage, without talent, resources
> or capacity to establish a third chain on this con-
> tinent. . . . In the second place, if such a Cana-
> dian non-commercial chain were constructed, it would
> seriously weaken the whole advertising basis of Cana-
> dian broadcasting. The question before this Commit-
> tee is whether Canada is to establish a chain that
> is owned and operated and controlled by Canadians,
> or whether it is to be owned and operated by commer-
> cial organizations associated with or controlled by
> American interests. The question is, the State or
> the United States?[10]

The history of Canada for the last century or more has, in
part, been an attempt to nurture a distinctive culture, in the
broad sense of that term. Indeed, it has probably been believed by people concerned about such questions that only when
Canada had developed a distinctive way of life, or culture in
a broad sense, would it produce culture in the more restricted
sense of works of imagination and intellect. In view of this
fact, it is perhaps useful to take a brief historical look at
the discussion of the nature of the Canadian culture or identity. Until fairly recently that discussion turned on the not
always very precise distinction that Frederick Philip Grove was
attempting to draw when he counterpoised "Europe" and "America."
Was Canada's true culture to be found in preserving inherited
"Europeanness" or in developing its "North Americanness"?

*   *   *

There was a time, not so many years ago, when to speak of Canada as a North American nation was viewed, at least in some quarters, as a heresy. In 1933 John W. Dafoe, editor of the Winnipeg Free Press, delivered a series of lectures at Columbia University in New York, which were subsequently published under the title Canada: An American Nation. He worried somewhat about the problem of a title for reasons which he explained in a letter to a friend:

> As a general title, I have had from such thought
> as I have been able to give to it, no luck. If I
> thought Mexico would not regard it as a casus belli,
> I might suggest "North America's Other Democracy."
> "America's Other Democracy" is more accurate but very
> flat. "Canada -- A North American Democracy" might
> earn me a lambasting from my imperialistic friends,
> but I am hardened to this usage.[11]

Dafoe was here engaged in a polemical practice which has a long and honoured tradition among nationalists in Canada: branding people whose conception of Canada differed from his with a pejorative tag. The dirtiest word in his vocabulary was "imperialist," a description Dafoe applied to virtually anyone who did not wish to see Canada's relations with Great Britain defined in exactly the fashion that he wished. These people, usually loyal Canadian nationalists themselves, would, of course, have replied in kind, denying to those who thought like Dafoe the worthy title of "nationalist" and branding him a "continentalist." These three terms, "nationalist," "imperialist," and "continentalist," have a fairly long history in Canadian political usage. Sometimes they have been used as terms of abuse, but at others they have been uttered as compliments. If the word "internationalist" is added to them, and it too has been both a term of denigration and approbation, a good deal of Canadian political discourse could be analysed. I do not wish to enter into a long analysis of historical semantics at this point, but some discussion of the past is necessary if any serious attempt is to be made to assess the concept of Canada as a North American nation.

Dafoe's term, "Canada -- An American Nation," was a minor heresy in the 1930s and would still be to some Canadians today because of their conviction that an earlier term, one enshrined in our constitution, was more proper and accurate. That term was "British North America." Throughout most of the nineteenth century, and probably down to the end of the First World War, most English-speaking Canadians would have unhesitatingly asserted that their country, while North

American in geography and in many of its material characteristics, was nevertheless British in its cultural and political traditions.   There can be no doubt that by the time of Confederation in 1867, and certainly in the three or four decades afterwards, a national consciousness was developing among English-speaking Canadians. It expressed itself in, among other ways, a desire for Canada to achieve a status of greater equality with Great Britain, but within a united British Empire. It was this determination to achieve nationhood without rupturing the sacred unity of the Empire that caused later generations of Canadian nationalists to condemn these British North American nationalists as "imperialists." The Grants and Parkins and Denisons and Leacocks who wrote and spoke so eloquently about Canada's national aspirations within the British Empire in the thirty years before Versailles were, as Professor Carl Berger has so effectively shown, a variety of Canadian nationalists.[12]   Both Sir John A. Macdonald and Sir Robert Borden understood what these men were talking about and, to some degree, shaped their policies in keeping with similar assumptions.

Nor were these men mere sentimentalists yearning for a piece of the action in an age of the British Empire's ascendancy. No doubt, of course, there was something of this. But more important was their assessment both of the meaning of Canada's historical experience and of its strategic position in North America.   First of all, nineteenth-century Canadians were convinced that what differentiated them from the United States was that they had preserved British political institutions and adapted them to the demands of the North American environment. They believed that their evolutionary history was superior to the revolutionary experience of their southern neighbours. They further believed that the evolutionary and conservative record of the past was a good guide to the future. By preserving those British traditions they could move toward nationhood gradually, modifying but never rejecting Canada's relationship with Great Britain. Thus Canada could avoid many of the problems which they felt characterized the turbulent republic to the south.

Moreover, the preservation of the imperial tie had important strategic implications. A small country like Canada, standing in such close proximity to the United States, always lived under the threat of absorption. It must always be remembered that the nineteenth-century experience of Canadians included several bitter memories of relations with the United States: the War of 1812, a long series of border disputes, the ruptured relations of the Civil War years, and the inflated claims of the United States at the Washington Conference in 1871. In the nineteenth century that famous undefended frontier had yet to be discovered.[13] The very existence of Canada, most nineteenth-century Canadians realized, was an anti-American fact. And for the preservation of that fact the association with Great Britain obviously had to be maintained. The British garrisons in Canada and the British Navy on the seas provided Canada's major military defence. These, of course, were defences of last resort; Canadians already believed that their best defence lay in Anglo-American amity.

Finally, it should never be forgotten that until the First World War Canada relied heavily on British capital, technology, and markets in developing its industrial and agricultural economy. Many of the largest developmental projects in Canada -- the Canadian Pacific Railway, for example -- were financed with the aid of British capital. In 1914, 75 per cent of all foreign capital in Canada came from British sources. Nor should one ignore the fact that the greatest source of immigration to Canada during the nineteenth century was the British Isles. Thus the close relationship with Britain that was implied in the concept of Canada as a "British North American nation" was based on strategic and material factors as well as historic and sentimental reasons.

By the end of the century, however, perceptible changes were already beginning to take place. Indeed, even during the nineteenth century, it seems almost unnecessary to remark, there was a significant element in the Canadian population which already thought of itself as essentially North American and displayed a rather detached attitude toward Great Britain. These, of course, were the French-speaking Canadians who were British subjects neither by birth, by political tradition, nor, to any great extent, by economic interest. They were British subjects by conquest. This is not to suggest that they were anti-British. Indeed, they tended to look on the British as generous conquerors who had, after a struggle, permitted them to remain themselves. Their tradition was strongly monarchist, and they saw the value of British support in preserving Canada's separate status in North America. The French Canadian's loyalty to the British Empire should have been unquestioned (though it was not always), provided it was understood that their responsibilities to the Empire related exclusively to the defence and development of that part of the Empire in which they lived.

Those who did not understand this fact should -- though most did not -- have learned it from the Boer War experience.

While English Canadians like Principal Grant of Queen's University or John Willison of the Toronto Globe could logically argue from their assumptions that Canadian participation in South Africa was a Canadian national responsibility, few French Canadians would have agreed. Neither Henri Bourassa nor Sir Wilfrid Laurier saw it that way, though Laurier was eventually forced to find a middle position: "limited participation in the Boer War, but not necessarily participation in all Imperial Wars." What the French Canadian, who had no ties with France comparable to those of English Canadians with Britain, was really saying in 1899 was that Canada, despite membership in the Empire, was a North American nation. While many English-speaking Canadians wished to see Canada's national status affirmed by the assumption of greater responsibility within the Empire, for the French Canadian, Canada gained national status by rejecting those responsibilities and affirming its autonomous status as a nation in North America. Armand Lavergne, a rising officer in Henri Bourassa's nationalist army, spoke for a long and well-established tradition when he told the Canadian Military Institute in 1910:

> Now I wish you to understand that although the French Canadians may differ with you in many ways and means on the subject of "National Defence," there is one thing you must not forget, and that is, that the spirit of the French Canadians is the same today as in 1775 and 1812. The Nationalists of Quebec today are willing and ready to give their last drop of blood for the defence of the British flag and British institutions in this country.

And he concluded, in case any of his enthusiastic audience had missed the point about "in this country," by asserting that, "We are loyal just as you are, but we understand that our duty as Canadians, and as part of the Empire is to build up a strong Canada by preparing in Canada a strong national defence."[14]

After 1900 several new factors entered the equation on what might be called the North American side. In the first place it had never been true that all English Canadians accepted British North American assumptions about Canada. Some, notably such Liberals as Edward Blake and Richard Cartwright, had begun in the 1880s to argue for closer relations with the United States, hoping to renegotiate the reciprocal trade agreement which the United States had abrogated in 1866. Even Sir John A. Macdonald, a British North American always, had never shown any enthusiasm for the formal schemes of imperial federation that were frequently discussed. Then the decision in the Alaska boundary dispute in 1903 was interpreted by many Canadians as a betrayal of Canada's interests by Britain -- and that only a few years after Canada had responded so gallantly to Britain's call for aid in South Africa.

To this was added the weight of a vast new immigrant population that arrived in Canada between 1900 and 1914. Only about one-third of these people came from the British Isles, with the majority moving from the United States or Europe. It could not be expected that many of these newcomers would have any powerful sentimental attachment to Great Britain -- many may have had the opposite feeling, wanting to leave Europe behind them. In any event, these people, who formed a large segment of the newly opened Canadian West, became a sympathetic audience for those who argued for the affirmation of Canada's North American character. That explains why some leading British Canadian nationalists, including Stephen Leacock, were immigration restrictionists.

A further factor, which before 1914 was only beginning to be felt, was the changing character of the Canadian economy. While British investment, largely in the form of bonds and loans, remained dominant,[15] American investment was growing. Furthermore, as several observers noted at the time, U.S. investment was different: it was not in the form of bonds and loans, it was direct investment which carried ownership and control with it. Moreover, these investments frequently took place in sectors of the Canadian economy (natural resources, in particular) where major markets were to be found most frequently in the United States. It is one of the unfortunate ironies of Canadian economic policy in the years between Confederation and the First World War that many of the measures designed to develop and protect a Canadian national economy, and to create jobs at home for Canadians, had the effect of encouraging U.S. investors to move directly into Canada either to escape the effects of the Canadian tariff against the United States or to gain the advantages of the British preference.[16] Although the shift from an economy oriented toward Britain and Europe to one oriented toward U.S. markets and capital was not completed until the 1920s, the trend was already becoming evident by 1914.[17]

Moreover, as U.S. capital moved into Canada, so too did American labour organizations, specifically the American Federation of Labor (AFL). These unions came, frequently on the invitation of Canadian workers, to help in the formation

of unions and to win better wages and working conditions for
Canadians. Their contribution was substantial. But it is
also true that they brought with them the Gompers pattern
and philosophy of union organization and gradually took control of the Trades and Labor Congress (TLC) of Canada. After
1902, with the triumph of the AFL unions in the TLC, the
Canadian union movement became, from the perspective of AFL
headquarters in Washington, just another "state federation of
labour." Here was the beginning of the fragmentation of the
Canadian labour movement, which might have developed along an
east-west axis but was, like the Canadian economy itself,
shifting in a continentalist direction.[18] In the 1930s the
story was repeated, with some variations in the field of industrial unions. The CIO union organizers, who had plenty to
keep them busy in the United States, came to Canada with considerable reluctance. But once they came they rapidly established their dominance. By 1950, in the words of Pat Conroy,
its Secretary-Treasurer, the Canadian Congress of Labour (the
CCL) had been reduced "to the status of a satellite organization."[19] Thus a major institution of a modern industrial society, the trade union movement, had become very much North
American and indeed continentalist in its orientation. One
consequence of this development, though it is also attribut-
able to other causes, was the emergence of a separate union
movement among a large number of French Canadian workers --
the Catholic syndicate.[20] From the viewpoint of the workers,
of course, these developments may have been a necessary response to their most immediate needs. But from the perspective of the trade union movement as an institution of national
integration, the implications are obvious enough.

It is interesting to note that the story of farmers' organizations in Canada is a rather different one. There has,
of course, been fragmentation between, for example, the Canadian Council of Agriculture, with its provincial sections, and
the Union Catholique des Cultivateurs. So, too, the influence
of American ideas on Canadian agricultural movements, from the
Grange to cooperativism, has been extensive.[21] But Canadian
farmers, while willing to learn from their American counterparts, have always preserved their independence. Perhaps the
reason is that Canadian agriculture developed in competition
with U.S. agricultural products, while the industrial and natural resources component of the Canadian economy has developed
more as an adjunct to its southern counterpart.

Beyond agricultural and labour organizations every demo-
cratic society spawns a multiplicity of voluntary organizations: professional, social, intellectual, and athletic.

Whether these are organizations of medical doctors, Kiwanians, political scientists, or hockey players, they can play a role in national integration. There are very few studies of such organizations in Canada, but a necessarily superficial observation suggests that many of these organizations have become continental in direction rather than simply Canada-wide. Rotary Clubs are an example; the Canadian Clubs are not. The Canadian Historical Association is independent, but many historians in Canada do not belong to it or, for a variety of reasons, also belong to, say, the American Historical Association. The same is probably true of political scientists, physicists, architects, and teachers of language and literature. In any final assessment of continental influences in Canada, a full study of these voluntary organizations would have to be made. Such associations could conceivably be as significant as, for example, the direction in which the Canadian economy or foreign affairs outlook has developed. My guess would be, and it is only a guess, that these informal associations between Canada and the United States have rapidly grown since 1914 while similar contacts with Britain and Europe have probably declined.

Even before World War I there was already considerable concern about the Americanization process that was perceived to be taking place. The periodicals of the time carried numerous articles with titles like "The Effect of the American Invasion," "Our Industrial Invasion of Canada," and "The Americanization of the Canadian Northwest."[22] J. Castell Hopkins, a prolific writer and ardent exponent of closer imperial unity, described the situation in this way in 1908:

> If the bosom of the future should hold a destiny of
> Canada apart from the British Empire, if the cher-
> ished ideal of loyal British peoples around the globe
> should never be realized and separation rather than
> closer union become a fact, it will be due in no
> small measure to the present day Americanization
> of Canadian thought, Canadian habits, Canadian lit-
> erature and the Canadian press. By this I do not
> mean the creation of an annexation sentiment. In-
> deed, the process I referred to is going on side by
> side with the growth of still more vigorous opposi-
> tion to continental union. It is rather the gradual
> but steady development of a non-British view of
> things; a situation in which public opinion here
> regarding the heart of the Empire and Imperial po-
> licy is formed along the lines of United States
> opinion, and therefore of an alien viewpoint.[23]

Most English Canadians would probably have argued that Canada was a British country in the years before 1914, but that assertion of Canadian Britishness sometimes had a curious twist. Howard Ferguson, whose logic was by no means his strongest suit, used this interesting argument in attacking French-language schools in Ontario in a speech in 1911. "This is a British country and we must maintain it as such if we are to maintain the high destiny that Providence intended for Canada," he told his constituents. "The bilingual system encourages the isolation of races. It impresses the mind of youth with the idea of race distinction and militates against the fusion of the various elements that make up our population. . . . The experience of the United States where their national school system recognizes but one language simply proves the wisdom of the system."[24] Was Ferguson saying that the best way to remain British was to adopt American educational policies? (Lord Durham had once warned of this element in English Canadian thinking. "Lower Canada must be English at the expense, if necessary, of not being British," he reported an informant as having told him.)[25] That was what Henri Bourassa detected: "Thanks to the campaign against the French language the English provinces are becoming Americanized rapidly," he claimed in 1916. "Toronto the loyal, Toronto the royal. Yankee Toronto, Yankee in its tastes, Yankee in its habits -- those who protest their loyalty loudest are least loyal at heart."[26]

During the age of Laurier much of the political controversy in both domestic and external affairs had turned on the highly emotional question of the essential character of Canada: British or North American. The inconclusive debate over imperial defence was fundamentally a discussion of that issue. So, too, was the perennial question of some form of reciprocal trade agreement with the United States. Intellectually in English Canada, the British Canadians were doubtless predominant -- the Grants, Parkins, Leacocks, and Macphails. But their position of pre-eminence was increasingly challenged by the Ewarts, Dafoes, and Skeltons of the North American school. And French Canadians have long since opted for North America. It took that perceptive Frenchman André Siegfried to raise the fundamental question just at the time that Europe was collapsing into war in the autumn of 1914. "Moeurs américaines, loyalisme Britannique!" Siegfried wrote. "Tout le problème de l'avenir politique canadien me parait résumé dans ces deux termes. Est-il possible en effet qu'américain de moeurs le Dominion reste politiquement Britannique?"[27]

The First World War, in which Canada participated with such effectiveness, at such enormous cost, is the pivotal

event in the transformation of Canada from a British North
American to an American nation. There is no doubt that in
September 1914 the British North Americans carried the day.
Just as the American nation to the south had few reasons to
doubt that its interests were best served by remaining aloof
from the European war, the British North American nation in
the north was equally convinced that its responsibility was
best expressed in Laurier's "Ready, Aye Ready." J. W. Dafoe,
a westerner with an increasingly North American outlook,
favoured unlimited participation. Henri Bourassa, a consistent critic of Canadian involvement in imperial affairs, was
prepared to go along, though not perhaps in an unlimited
fashion. Yet as the war dragged on, bringing increasingly
high casualty rates, profound internal divisions, and fre-
quent irritations with British conduct of the war, a growing
number of Canadians appeared to have had serious doubts about
too intimate relations with the Empire and Europe. Moreover,
once the United States entered the war, old animosities which
had already been disappearing seemed to vanish.

It was Sir Robert Borden, for instance, who is often
viewed as an "imperialist" working for closer imperial ties,
who moved unsuccessfully to establish the first Canadian
diplomatic representation at Washington. It also was Borden
who expressed himself before the Imperial War Cabinet in
1918 in a profoundly North American fashion. "Future good
relations between ourselves and the United States were, as
he had said before, the best asset we could bring home from
the war. . . . He wished . . . to make it clear that if the
future policy of the British Empire meant working in co-
operation with some European nation as against the United
States, that policy could not reckon on the approval or support of Canada."[28] Borden was here expressing a sentiment
which perhaps most Canadians, irrespective of party or ethnic
background, would have accepted. Certainly it was the underlying assumption of Canadian foreign policy between the wars,
whether that policy was set by Arthur Meighen on the matter
of the Anglo-Japanese Alliance in 1921, by R. B. Bennett
during the Manchurian crisis of 1931, or Mackenzie King
from Chanak in 1922 to Munich in 1938. And of their critics,
those who preached internationalism, like J. W. Dafoe,
were probably less influential than those who, like J. S.
Woodsworth or Henri Bourassa, called for a more thorough-
going isolationism.

North American isolationism, which meant drawing closer
to the United States, aroused few fears among Canadians. The
United States had been our ally during the war and that seemed

to erase all the lingering fears of "manifest destiny" and the "big stick." Sir William Peterson, Principal of McGill University and a long-time "imperialist," expressed the new spirit when the Americans entered the war in 1917. "It has also done something," he wrote in that confident rhetoric so characteristic of university presidents, "to consolidate the interests of the English-speaking peoples, and to hasten the day when a mutual understanding between Britain and America will bring with it an effectual guarantee for the peace and prosperity of all mankind."[29] That was the sentiment that was to prevail after the war.

Very few Canadians would have taken seriously Archibald MacMechan's article in an early number of the Canadian Historical Review in 1920, entitled "Canada as a Vassal State." In seven pages he summed up all of the ways in which Canada had become bound to the United States -- everything from investment and sport to chewing gum and Mother's Day were attributed to American influence. And here is what he said about Canadian universities at a date when hardly an American professor had yet stepped across the border. "The curriculum, text-books, methods of teaching, oversight of students, 'credits' are borrowed from the United States. Organization and administration are on the American Model. Among the students, American ideas prevail."[30] If MacMechan was right, most Canadians probably would have responded by asking for more. And that is what they got, whether they asked for it or not.

Canada's withdrawal from the Empire-Commonwealth -- for that in fact was what it was -- into fortress North America was partly the result of revulsion against Europe and its bloody battlefields. It was also the consequence of the conviction that Canada's internal problems, both developmental policies and the restoration of national unity, had to be given first priority. And finally, it reflected the further evolution of those trends in the Canadian economy that had already been evident before 1914. If a symbolic date is needed to mark the change, 1926 would be better than most.

There are many reasons for choosing this date, most of them well known. But there is a reason less often remarked upon, but which is very deserving of consideration. This was an important cultural event which revealed with great clarity the temper of the times. In 1926 a journalist named F. E. Hauser published a book entitled A Canadian Art Movement. The Story of the Group of Seven. Hauser's book is a vibrant expression of Canadian cultural nationalism, and it marks the apotheosis of the Group of Seven. In 1926 the Group was still basking in the warmth of its reception at the famous Wembley Exhibition of 1924. That had been a dual triumph. Not only had the Group's work received lavish praise from the English critics, but the Group's very presence at the exhibition marked the triumph of the new artists over the traditionalist and European-oriented painters of the Royal Canadian Academy.[31] It was Hauser's task to delineate the elements of the nationalism which the Group so consciously sought to create. The job was not too difficult, for several of the painters, notably A. Y. Jackson, Arthur Lismer, and Lawren Harris, had frequently explained their conception of Canadian nationalism. But Hauser succeeded perhaps better than any of them had ever done:

> Our British and European connection in fact, so far as creative expression in Canada is concerned, has been a millstone about our neck . . . As long as Canada regarded herself artistically as a mere outpost of Europe; so long as her painters elected for voluntary mediocrity by the mental admission that Canadians possessed no potentialities with which to create a culture as good or better than Europe's; so long was our 20th Century born spirit of independence voiceless. . . . For Canada to find a complete racial expression of herself through art, a complete break with European traditions was necessary; a new type of artist was required, a type with sufficient creative equipment to initiate of its own through handling new materials by new methods and what was required more than technique was a deep-rooted love of the country's natural environment. . . . The message that the Group of Seven art movement gives to this age is the message that here in the North has arisen a young nation with faith in its own creative genius.[32]

Hauser quite accurately saw that the Group of Seven was a painters' movement which had turned its back on Europe. Canadian painting had to be about Canada. Both form and content had to be distinctive. And so the "Hot Mush School" was born. The school's triumph over adversity was certainly much easier than Hauser allowed, and it was complete by 1926. Indeed it might be argued that the Group's triumph at Wembley in 1924 was at least as revealing of what was happening to Canada as was Mackenzie King's success in 1923 at the Imperial Conference. The message of the Group was simply that, culturally, Canada was a North American nation. These new painters had come, in Lawren Harris' words, "to realize how far this country of Canada was different in character, atmosphere, moods, and spirit from Europe and the old land."[33] What F. E. Hauser did was to provide the Group with one of the elements necessary to any nationalist movement: a history.

Since politics imitates art, it is not surprising that 1926 is better known as the date marking some events of a more prosaic character than the triumph of the Group of Seven. The first of these is the declaration of the Imperial Conference of 1926, which provided the theoretical explanation for the autonomy of the dominions within the British Commonwealth. The dominions were now recognized as nations in the traditional sense of having the right to control fully both internal and external policies. For Canada, however, the date has another perhaps more profound, though frequently ignored, significance. After 1926 American investment in Canada exceeded British investment, and Canada's major economic axis was moving increasingly in a north-south direction.[34]

The shift in the source and kind of foreign investment did not pass unobserved in 1926. Bank publications and the Financial Post took note of the change. The Canadian Forum, which in the interwar years was the intellectual organ of the North American trend in Canadian nationalism, published a sober analysis entitled "The Penetration of American Capital in Canada." The author was interested not only in the economic aspects of this development, but also in the potential political consequences. Though fully aware of Scott Nearing's arguments for the view that the flag follows investment, the author rejected them:

> In the first place the Dominion is not a backward country peopled by a race indifferent to the development of their country; but, on the contrary, an energetic nation of ambitious thrifty people. The government is stable, the people politically minded and not the dupes or blind followers of vain leaders. In the second place, although Canada is not a power of the first rank itself, yet it is part of the British Empire and thus enjoys the prestige and strength of Great Britain. This nullifies any idea of annexation of Canada by force. There is still the possibility that American capital may secretly buy up the newspapers, endow the churches and universities, and begin a careful education of the public to the idea that annexation to the United States would be the course for best development. . . . But

the loyalty to the British connection, which is
so striking and refreshing a feature of Canadian history, would act as an effective counter
weight to such propaganda unless this country
was in the midst of severe economic distress.[35]

Three months after these lines were published, in November
1926, the first Canadian minister was appointed to Washington, something which those who thought of themselves as
British North Americans had long resisted.[36]

Given these developments, it is perhaps not too unfair
to suggest that another event which took place in these years
was more than a mere coincidence. This concerns a radical
alteration in military strategic thought. Since the military establishment was small, the importance of this development should not be exaggerated. But it is of interest. In
1920 Colonel J. Sutherland Brown was appointed Director of
Military Operations and Intelligence. "Buster" Brown may be
taken as an illustration of the adage that military men are
always preparing to fight the last war -- in this instance
the War of 1812. In any case, as Professor Eayrs has pointed
out, Brown's Defence Scheme No. 1 argued that strategic planning should be based on the assumption that the major military threat to Canadian security came from the United States.
Whatever significance was attached to Defence Scheme No. 1,
it lapsed into obsolescence with Brown's transfer to another
post in 1927 and was officially cancelled in 1931.[37] Here
was a clear sign of the times, and one which revealed some
important assumptions about the "fire-proof house" theory of
Canadian security that prevailed in the interwar years.

It was another university president, this time from
Toronto, who perhaps best summed up the spirit that was
abroad in Canada by the mid-twenties. Sir Robert Falconer,
in a series of lectures delivered in England in 1925 under
the title of "The United States as a Neighbour," explained
effectively the basis of the close relations that existed
between Canada and the United States. Canada, in effect,
had become a northern extension of the republic, and that
seemed a happy enough circumstance to Falconer. After all,
"Americans of Anglo-Saxon origin and English-speaking Canadians are more alike than any other separate people." That,
of course, left out a lot of Americans, to say nothing at
all of nearly 50 per cent of Canadians! Economics, geography,
and communications had drawn the two nations together, and
American education, especially graduate education, was enor-
mously important to Canada. "It is from the American

university chiefly," the Toronto president remarked, "that this health giving influence is coming in like a refreshing breeze." Nor could his series end without a rhetorical flourish about the mission of Canada. Once more Canada's special place in cementing the moral unity of the English-speaking world was trotted out. It may sound platitudinous now, but once that was a mission that made Canadians proud, for it was the essence of their nationalism: It gave Canada a uniqueness which, at the same time, could serve all mankind. In Falconer's concluding words:

> A review of the history of the relations between the United States and Canada affords encouragement to those who believe that a better day will come for the world when all the branches of the English-speaking peoples work in sympathy with one another. . . . If ever a new order is to be ushered in, the day will certainly begin with the creation of sympathy between them. For the hastening of such a day Canada, in her history, her character and her position holds a unique privilege and, if she takes advantage of it, the world of the future will judge that she will have played a part given to few nations in the progress of humanity.[38]

No book on Canadian humour should be without a section devoted to the predictions of Canadian nationalists!

Men who thought like Falconer shaped Canadian policy in the interwar years. Their first assumption was that increasingly the interests of Canada and those of the United States were the same, and that these interests differed from those of Britain and Europe. The second assumption, one which Franklin Roosevelt and Mackenzie King expressed in speeches at Kingston and Woodbridge, Ontario, in August of 1938, was that the United States would defend Canada against external aggression. Here, then, are the roots of a common North American defence policy.

There is, however, more to the story. As Europe lapsed into war again in the late 1930s, Canada was placed in a particularly difficult position. Despite the isolationist mood of the country, there were nevertheless many Canadians who were prepared to go to war again to fight the Nazis or to aid Britain. This sentiment not only threatened the internal unity of the country but also threatened to disrupt Canadian-American relations for, as a popular book of the time put it, "Canada compromises America's isolation."[39]

These factors, plus a third one, provided the rationale for the heavy Canadian involvement in the North American defence system which has been a foundation of Canadian policy since the Second World War -- the Permanent Joint Board on Defence, the Defence Production Sharing Agreements, and NORAD. That third factor, sometimes ignored by critics of the wartime agreements, was that after 1939 both Britain and Canada became convinced that the Axis powers could only be defeated if the United States was brought into the war. Thus Canada's involvement with the United States must be seen as part of an effort to nudge its southern neighbour into fuller support for the Allied cause. This is what underlay persistent platitudes of Mackenzie King and other Canadians about Canada's role as a "linchpin" or "bridge" between Britain and the United States. Here the whole theory of the "North Atlantic Triangle" and the "moral unity of the English-speaking world," so dear to Canadians since at least the 1890s, was being worked out in practice.[40] At the end of the war King recorded in his diary words that simply echoed Sir Robert Borden's sentiments of 1918. Returning from England in November 1945, King observed in his sanctimonious way, "It is hard to believe it is not part of some larger design to help in keeping the English-speaking peoples together and of furthering international good-will at a time when that would seem to be more necessary even than before the beginning of the last Great War."[41]

This Canadian role of bridge has, of course, always been partly a myth. It is true that as long as the United States remained neutral it was possible to act as something of a go-between. But that did not last long, and King was probably more realistic some years later when he described his role at the Quebec Conference: "I was, as you recall, not so much a participant in any of the discussions as a sort of general host, whose task at the Citadel was similar to that of the General Manager of the Chateau Frontenac."[42] The fact surely is that the North Atlantic Triangle was never an equilateral -- Canada was always a minor leg, and by 1945 the British side was also rapidly shrinking. As has frequently been observed, after 1940 Canada, which for twenty years had been affirming its North American character, found itself alone in North America alongside a gigantic American partner which was about to assume the role of policeman in a world passing rapidly from hot to cold war.

The Cold War ensured that the alliance system established during World War II would be maintained and strengthened. NATO was a multilateral arrangement which helped re-

dress the balance against American might. But in North
America multilateralism gave way to bilateralism, with NORAD
being added to the earlier arrangements in 1958. Once again
Canada set out into a period of massive internal development,
again heavily financed by American direct investment: $4.9
billion of American capital were invested in Canada in 1945,
and that had increased nearly fourfold by 1963. While sta-
tistics do not tell the whole story, the Task Force on Foreign Ownership and the Structure of Canadian Industry reported
in 1968 that U.S. investors controlled 97 per cent of the
capital in the automobile industry, 90 per cent in rubber, 54
per cent in electrical equipment. Foreign, largely U.S.,
ownership and control reached 62 per cent in mining and smelt-
ing and 74 per cent in oil and natural gas.[43] If all business
assets are considered, only about 27 per cent were foreign
controlled in 1968, and it is at least possible that the percentage has levelled off and may even be declining.[44]

Nor do investment figures tell the whole story. Increasingly, the United States had become the major market for
Canadian products, particularly the new mineral and oil sta-
ples. And some sections of the Canadian economy, such as the
automobile industry, had become fully integrated into a continental system. This, plus the pegged relationship of the
Canadian and U.S. dollars, ensured that the Canadian economy
became highly sensitive to economic fluctuations within the
United States. So close had this relationship become that in
1965 one perceptive, if gloomy, Canadian, Professor George
Grant, was prepared to pronounce a lament on the death of a
Canada gobbled up in continentalism.[45] Three years later,
Mr. George Ball, former Under Secretary in the U.S. State De-
partment, offered a somewhat similar prognostication:

> Sooner or later, commercial imperatives will
> bring about the free movement of all goods back
> and forth across our long border. When that
> occurs, or even before it does, it will become
> unmistakably clear that countries with economies
> inextricably intertwined must also have free
> movement of the other vital factors of produc-
> tion -- capital, services, labour. The result
> will inevitably be substantial economic inte-
> gration, which will require for its full real-
> ization a progressively expanding area of common
> political decision.[46]

Nor was this problem an economic one alone. In 1950,
the Report of the Royal Commission on the Arts, Letters and

<u>Sciences</u> warned of the growing impact of American culture
on Canada. A similar concern was expressed by the 1957
<u>Report of the Royal Commission on Broadcasting</u>. In 1961
the O'Leary Commission on Publications observed that

> The tremendous expansion of communications in the
> United States has given that nation the world's
> most penetrating and effective apparatus for the
> transmission of ideas. Canada, more than any
> other country, is naked to that force, exposed un-
> ceasingly to a vast network of communications
> which reaches to every corner of our land; Ameri-
> can words, images and print -- the good, the bad,
> the indifferent -- batter unrelentingly at our
> eyes and ears.[47]

Added to this concern with cultural continentalism have been
more recent expressions of anxiety about the substantial percentage of United States citizens who have been employed in
Canadian universities, and the expanding sector of the Canadian publishing industry which has been taken over by U.S.
firms, and even growing American domination of the Canadian
sporting scene, as exemplified by the expansion of the National Hockey League.[48] By 1970, a growing number of Canadians were prepared to admit that there was a large element
of truth in Harold Innis' remark in 1948 that Canada had
"moved from colony to nation to colony."[49]

The causes of this condition of dependence -- some would
call it colonialism -- are numerous and complex. The easiest
attitude is to attribute it to an amorphous, undefined state
called "colonial mindedness." This state of mind manifests
itself in the belief that others can always do things better
than we can and therefore we Canadians should either copy the
initiatives of others, or let them do our tasks for us. That
this condition exists cannot be denied, though it is not as
widespread as is sometimes suggested in the rhetoric of the
most ardent critics of our national inferiority complex. But
even to the extent that it does exist, it is less a cause
than an effect of our condition.

One of the most obvious reasons for Canadian dependence
is simply size and geography: twenty million people living
beside two hundred million can hardly expect to be equals,
especially when the larger community is as technologically
advanced and economically powerful as the United States is.
Nor is it surprising, given the example of American afflu-
ence and power at their doorstep, that many Canadians should

both aspire to a similar standard of life and become convinced that the way to achieve it is through adopting American techniques. There is a large element of truth, and irony,
in Professor Mel Watkins' argument that even Macdonald's "national policies" of the 1870s and 1880s were copied from an
American patent.[50] The difficulty was that without some serious and determined effort to stimulate and develop Canadian
capital formation, technological innovation, and entrepreneurship, the adoption of the United States model almost inevitably brought with it the need for American and other
foreign parts to make the model work. As Professor Watkins
once remarked, "high tariffs and lavish railway subsidies
expressed the limits of political action, while, significantly, education, particularly business schools, and freer banking -- which might have facilitated the rise of new domestic
entrepreneurs -- were neglected."[51]

     The same proposition might be tested in the context of
many other aspects of Canadian life: the military establishment where American weaponry, sometimes of a somewhat obso-
lete kind, is dominant; the mass media where Disneyland,
Sesame Street, and the Beverly Hillbillies make Canadian as
well as American cash registers ring; and in Canadian education, where everything from John Dewey to Jerry Rubin has
made its impact. The theme is one that runs through much of
John Porter's controversial but penetrating study, The
Vertical Mosaic. Porter places special emphasis on the fail-
ure of Canada's educational system to keep pace with the "kind
of society that has been emerging during the century."[52] Too
frequently, when Canadians lacked the skills demanded by modern industrial society, governments have relied upon skilled
immigrants, who were relatively cheap, rather than entered
upon the expensive business of upgrading Canadians through
education. Skilled immigrants from the United States have
frequently been among the most readily available. (There is
an ironic twist to Porter's argument which might be noted in
passing. His contention is that the very conservative and
status-conscious character which has distinguished us from
the upwardly mobile melting pot to the south, is what has
forced Canadians to rely on outside initiatives for many of
its dynamic developments. In other words, Canada has fallen
under American domination because it has not adopted American values!)[53]

     The controversy over the large number of foreign citi-
zens who teach in Canadian universities[54] can partly be
explained in Porter's terms. The large-scale expansion of
higher education in Canada since the 1950s, made necessary

by population growth, rising aspirations, and economic demand, was largely possible because of the availability of well-trained scholars and teachers from other countries, particularly the United States where the importance of highly expensive post-graduate education had long since been recognized. The Canadian alternative would have been a massive, and costly, crash programme to educate Canadians, and even this would have necessitated sending many Canadians abroad for specialized education. Instead, the undergraduate bulge came first, followed only later by a modest expansion of graduate education. To fill the gap, Canadian universities employed a large number of foreign professors. Today we have relatively large graduate programmes educating qualified Canadians at a time when undergraduate numbers appear to be levelling off or declining, and when educational expenditures are increasingly resented by the taxpayer. The result will almost certainly be a number of frustrated, underemployed Canadians unable to find university positions. This will be followed by cutbacks in expenditures in graduate education. When, and if, the next bulge comes in higher education, we will doubtless again be found frantically searching abroad for more professors.[55]

Whatever side one takes in the controversy over foreign professors in Canadian universities, it is difficult to escape two conclusions. First, the situation is one of our own making, and it was made for reasons that appeared good, or at least necessary, at the time. Second, what has happened in our universities illustrates, in microcosm, a process which has taken place in many segments of Canadian society. The desire to keep up with our affluent neighbour, combined with the unwillingness or inability to pay the price, has meant increased dependence upon the United States. There is, after all, no such thing as a free lunch.

Obviously, there are many other reasons for the growing continental influence on Canada. Many economists, including those who composed the report of the Watkins task force, have criticized the structure of Canadian industry and public policies governing the industrial sector of the economy. Tariffs, antitrust policies, and certain features of our tax laws have reduced competitive performance and encouraged foreign take-overs. Then, too, there is the difficulty which Canadian businessmen sometimes experience in obtaining funds for expansion -- funds more readily available to prospective United States buyers who have the strong backing of giant multinational assets.[56] Finally, there is the often decried, but never fully explained, conservatism of Canadian investors, who apparently favour blue chip stocks in the United States to riskier Canadian ventures.

Canadians have worried about this drift toward continentalism for many years; the concern is almost as old as the country itself.[57] Royal commission has followed royal commission, and these in turn have been followed by task forces, parliamentary investigations, and endless debate. But whether for ideological reasons, lack of will, conflicting vested interests, varying regional needs, or just plain lack of imagination, only a few definite policies have emerged out of the clouds of rhetoric. A CBC, a CRTC, a Canada Council, and even a Canada Development Corporation have been put in place. The impact of these institutions, though important, is hardly the equal of the vast and apparently attractive power of continental drift. In a society like Canada, which is still gripped by an ideology of developmentalism and growthmanship, perhaps the drift is inevitable -- especially when significant segments of the population have yet to experience the advantages of the affluent society.

All that being said, and perhaps even partly explained in the calm manner that becomes an historian, one pertinent fact remains: Having become a North American nation, many Canadians are unhappy or at least uneasy. They now realize that simply casting off European encumbrances has not resulted in the emergence of a distinctly Canadian culture. Indeed, there is more than a suspicion that becoming North American has meant becoming American -- or almost. Canadian Senate committees are rarely alarmist, yet one such committee studying the mass media concluded in 1970 that: "Cultural survival is perhaps the most critical problem our generation of Canadians will have to face, and it may be it can be achieved only by using all the means at our command."[58]

Many Canadians, though it is impossible to say how many, share that opinion though there are differences about the nature and disposition of "the means at our command." Yet one thing seems fairly certain: Canadians are anxious to make their own decisions about the future development of their culture and polity. Making your own decisions, after all, is itself an evidence of a distinctive national culture. And that explains why many Canadians resent the assumption underlying the recent comment, doubtless made with friendly intent, by Mr. Thomas Enders, the United States Ambassador to Canada, to the effect that "Canadians want to be less dependent, less focused upon the U.S. We encourage them in that. But we want them to do it in a positive way -- by building new ties with other countries rather than just loosening their ties with us."[59]

The wellspring of cultural nationalism in Canada has always been the desire to make our own judgments about what is best for us, about what policies are negative or positive. Today, as in the nineteenth century, in a world of nations, it remains true that self-government is always preferable to what someone else believes may be good government.

July 1976

NOTES

1. Frederick Philip Grove, "Nationhood," in his It Needs to Be Said (Toronto: 1929), p. 142.

2. Raymond Williams, Keywords. A Vocabulary of Culture and Society (London: Oxford University Press, 1976), p. 76.

3. Margaret Atwood, Survival (Toronto: House of Anansi Press, 1972).

4. Ramsay Cook, The Maple Leaf Forever (Toronto: Macmillan of Canada, 1970).

5. Robin Mathews and James Steele, The Struggle for Canadian Universities (Toronto: New Press, 1969). Michael Butler and David Shugarman, "Americanization and Scholarly Values," Journal of Canadian Studies, August 1970, pp. 12-27. Allan Kornberg and Alan Tharp, "The American Impact on Canadian Political Science and Sociology," in R. A. Preston, The Influence of the United States on Canadian Development (Durham: Duke University Press, 1972) pp. 55-98.

6. Wallace Clement, The Canadian Corporate Elite (Toronto: McClelland and Stewart, 1975).

7. Barry Lord, The History of Painting in Canada: Towards a People's Art (Toronto: NC Press, 1974).

8. Bruce Kidd and John Macfarlane, The Death of Hockey (Toronto: McClelland and Stewart, 1972).

9. S. M. Crean, Who's Afraid of Canadian Culture? (Toronto: General Publishing, 1976).

10. See Margaret Prang, "The Origins of Public Broadcasting in Canada," Canadian Historical Review, Vol. XLVI, No. 1 (March 1965), pp. 1-31.

11. Public Archives of Canada, Dafoe Papers, J. W. Dafoe to Dr. H. L. McBain, January 20, 1934.

12. C. C. Berger, The Sense of Power (Toronto: University of Toronto Press, 1969).

13. For a concise statement see C. P. Stacey, The Undefended Border: The Myth and the Reality (Ottawa: C.H.A. Histori-

cal booklets, 1954), and Robert Craig Brown, "Canada in North America," in John Braeman et al., 20th Century American Foreign Policy (Columbus: Ohio State University Press, 1971), pp. 343-77.

14. Armand Lavergne, "National Defence as Viewed by French Canadians," Canadian Military Institute, Selected Papers from the Transcriptions of the Canadian Military Institute, 1910 (Welland: 1910), pp. 98, 102.

15. F. W. Field, Capital Investments in Canada (Montreal: Monetary Times of Canada, 1914), pp. 9-35. A. J. deBray, L'Essor Industriel et Commercial du Peuple Canadien (Montreal: Beau Chemin, n.d.).

16. J. M. Bliss, "Canadianizing American Business: The Roots of Branch Plant," in Ian Lumsden, ed., Close the 49th Parallel (Toronto: University of Toronto Press, 1970), pp. 27-42. See also United States Tariff Commission, Reciprocity with Canada: A Study in the Arrangement of 1911 (Washington: GPO, 1911), p. 76.

17. For a thorough discussion see Hugh G. J. Aitken, American Capital and Canadian Resources (Cambridge: Harvard University Press, 1961).

18. Robert Babcock, "The A.F. of L. in Canada: A Study in Labour Imperialism" (unpublished Ph.D. thesis, Duke University, 1969).

19. Irving Abella, "American Unionism, Communism and the Canadian Labour Movement: Some Myths and Realities," in Preston, op. cit., cited on p. 223. See also I. M. Abella, "Lament for a Union Movement," in Lumsden, op. cit., pp. 75-92.

20. Alfred Charpentier, Ma Conversion au Syndicalisme Catholique (Montreal: Fides, 1946).

21. Paul Sharp, Agrarian Revolt in Western Canada (Minneapolis: University of Minnesota Press, 1948).

22. World's Work, September 1905; World's Work, January 1903 Cosmopolitan, April 1903.

23. J. Castell Hopkins, Continental Influences in Canadian Development (Toronto: 1908), p. 3.

24. Kempville Advance, December 7, 1911, cited in Peter Oliver, "The Making of a Provincial Premier: Howard Ferguson and Ontario Politics, 1870-1923" (unpublished Ph.D. thesis, University of Toronto, 1969), p. 134.

25. Sir Reginald Coupland, ed., The Durham Report (Oxford: Oxford University Press, 1945), p. 43.

26. The Citizen, Ottawa, June 26, 1916.

27. André Siegfried, Deux Mois en l'Amérique du Nord à la Veille de la Guerre (Paris: Armand Colin, 1916), p. 12.

28. Canada, Documents on External Affairs. II. The Paris Peace Conference of 1919, R. A. MacKay, ed. (Ottawa: Queen's Printer, 1969), p. 17.

29. W. P. [Sir William Peterson], "English-speaking Solidarity," The University Magazine, Vol. XVI (April 1917), p. 154.

30. Archibald MacMechan, "Canada as a Vassal State," Canadian Historical Review, Vol. I, No. 4 (December 1920), p. 350.

31. Peter Mellen, The Group of Seven (Toronto: McClelland and Stewart, 1970), p. 104. Anne Davis, "The Wembley Controversy in Canadian Art," Canadian Historical Review, Vol. XIV, No. 1 (March 1973).

32. F. E. Hauser, A Canadian Art Movement. The Story of the Group of Seven (Toronto: Macmillan, 1926), pp. 13, 16, 17, 215.

33. Lawren Harris, "The Group of Seven in Canadian History," Canadian Historical Association Report, 1948, p. 30. It is fairly clear that Harris thought not so much in terms of Canada vs. Europe, but rather of North America vs. Europe. In 1928 he wrote: "Just as we enter new relationships in space which evoke a new attitude and are giving rise to what we call the modern world, so there is a new race forming on this continent, the race of the new dispensation which will develop and embody the new attitude. It grows now largely within the swaddling clothes of European culture and tradition, but its ideals are not the same. Its attitude is not the same. Its direction is not the same, as both Lincoln and Whitman knew." Lawren Harris, "Creative Art and

Canada," in Bertram Brooker, Yearbook of the Arts in Canada, 1928-1929 (Toronto: Macmillan, 1929), p. 181.

34. Hugh G. J. Aitken, "The Changing Structure of the Canadian Economy," in Hugh G. J. Aitken et al., The American Economic Impact on Canada (Durham: Duke University Press, 1959), p. 7.

35. J. Margorie Van der Hoek, "The Penetration of American Capital in Canada," Canadian Forum, Vol. VI, No. 71 (August 1926), p. 335.

36. H. Gordon Skilling, Canadian Representation Abroad (Toronto: Ryerson Press, 1945), pp. 185-233.

37. James Eayrs, In Defence of Canada: From the Great War to the Great Depression (Toronto: University of Toronto Press, 1965), pp. 70-77.

38. Sir Robert Falconer, The United States as a Neighbour (London: Cambridge University Press, 1925), pp. 1, 242-51. The subject of U.S. influence on Canada was a popular one in the 1920s. W. B. Munro, in the Marfleet Lectures at the University of Toronto in 1929, later published as American Influences on Canadian Government (Toronto: Macmillan, 1929), summed up a widely accepted view this way: "It is inevitable, of course, that the influence of American political practise upon Canada should be far-reaching. The juxtaposition of a neighbour which so far outranges Canada in population, wealth and world importance means that every branch of Canadian life and thought must be subjected to an overwhelming psychological pressure from south of the line. American influence upon Canada is more powerful than all the foreign influences combined. American newspapers, periodicals and American motion pictures are daily carrying American political ideas into every hamlet in the Dominion. The radio will accentuate this pressure, for the broadcasting stations pay no heed to international boundaries. One might, perhaps, generalize by saying that in the government and politics of Canada most of what is superimposed is British, but most of what works its way in from the bottom is American." (pp. 90-91). Of course, some Canadians hoped to resist the "inevitable." See John C. Weaver, "Canadians Confront American Mass Culture, 1918-30" (unpublished paper presented to the Canadian Historical Association, June 1972). See also Carl Berger, "Internationalism, Con-

tinentalism and the Writing of History: Comments on the Carnegie Series and the Relations of Canada and the United States," in Preston, op. cit., pp. 32-54.

39. John MacCormac, Canada: America's Problem (New York: Viking Press, 1940), p. 13.

40. Ramsay Cook, "From Lord Grey to Lloyd George," International Journal, Vol. XXVI, No. 1 (Winter 1970), pp. 186-93.

41. J. W. Pickersgill and D. S. Forster, The Mackenzie King Record, III, 1945-1946 (Toronto: University of Toronto Press, 1970), p. 95. See also D. G. Creighton, "Canada in the English-speaking World," Canadian Historical Review, Vol. XXVI, No. 2 (June 1945), pp. 119-27.

42. W. L. M. King to Lord Moran, June 9, 1950, in Churchill; taken from the Diaries of Lord Moran: The Struggle for Survival 1940-1945 (Boston: Houghton Mifflin, 1966), p. 117, n. 3.

43. Canada, Privy Council Office, Foreign Ownership and the Structure of Canadian Industry (Ottawa: Queen's Printer, 1968), pp. 9-11.

44. A. E. Safarian, "Some Myths About Foreign Business Investment in Canada," Journal of Canadian Studies, Vol. VI, No. 3 (August 1971), pp. 3-20.

45. George Grant, Lament for a Nation (Toronto: McClelland and Stewart, 1965). Part of Grant's argument is anticipated by Frederick Philip Grove's essay "Nationhood," in It Needs to Be Said, pp. 133-63.

46. George Ball, The Discipline of Power (Boston: Little, Brown, 1968).

47. Report/Royal Commission on Publications (Ottawa: Queen's Printer, 1961), pp. 5-6.

48. For a catalogue of concerns, see the essays in Lumsden, op. cit.

49. Harold Adams Innis, Essays in Canadian Economic History (Toronto: University of Toronto Press, 1956), p. 405.

50. Mel Watkins, "The American System and Canada's National Policy," _Canadian Association of American Studies Bulletin_, Winter 1967.

51. Mel Watkins, "A New National Policy," in Trevor Lloyd and Jack McLeod, eds., _Agenda 1970_ (Toronto: University of Toronto Press, 1968), p. 163.

52. John Porter, _The Vertical Mosaic_ (Toronto: University of Toronto Press, 1965), p. 56.

53. John Porter, "Canadian Character in the 20th Century," _Annals of the American Academy of Political and Social Science_, No. 370 (March 1967), pp. 49-56.

54. Mathews and Steele, _op. cit_.

55. Eugene Benson, "The House that Davis Built," _C.A.U.T. Bulletin_, Vol. 19, No. 3 (Spring 1971), pp. 6-7.

56. Robert L. Perry, "Why Henry Lee Sold Foreign . . . ," _Financial Post_, September 25, 1971, pp. 30-32. See also _Foreign Direct Investment in Canada_ (Ottawa: Government of Canada, 1972) and Pierre L. Bourgault, _Innovation and the Structure of Canadian Industry_ (Ottawa: Science Council of Canada, 1972).

57. S. F. Wise and R. C. Brown, _Canada Views the United States_ (Seattle: University of Washington Press, 1967).

58. Canada, Parliament, _Report of the Special Senate Committee on the Mass Media_ (Ottawa: Government of Canada, 1970), p. 194.

59. _US News & World Report_, June 21, 1976, p. 67.

3.

REFLECTIONS ON QUEBEC'S CULTURAL NATIONALISM

Solange Chaput Rolland, O. C.

Cultural Nationalism

It has always seemed easier for an observer who is detached from
all manifestations of cultural nationalism to study its cause,
its consequences, and its effects on a society, an ethnic group,
a country. But, first, it is most important to define the words
culture and nationalism before attempting to legitimate their
raison d'être in French Canada and in Quebec.

Culture is nothing else than "la mémoire du peuple" -- a
people's memory, and an anticipation of its future. It is the
very essence of that part of man which is not material, which is
a longing for God. Nationalism is a feeling of belonging to a
group of people. It has many other connotations, many other
emotions -- even passions -- attached to it.

An American may speak proudly of nationalism. An English-
speaking Canadian will sneer at Quebec's nationalism because
instinctively he aligns it with separatism, but he will see
nothing specifically wrong in a law which prohibits Time magazine from being published in Canada by removing the legal pri-
vileges it hitherto enjoyed. He applauds the Canadian Radio-
Television Commission when it stipulates that all Canadian
programmes must reflect a Canadian point of view but will
criticize the French-language radio and television networks if
producers and directors wish to promote a Quebec point of view
rather than a North American or a Canadian way of life. These
examples only point out the differences of opinions, of judgments, which surround the two expressions, nationalism and
cultural nationalism.

An International Background

It is a normal reaction for Frenchmen, Englishmen, Germans, and Russians, I suppose, to view dimly all those who not only promote cultural nationalism but who live by it. For cultural nationalism is primarily a tool for smaller nations that share the same language and culture with more important ones; it is a "réflexe de défense." Belgians and Quebecers react to French culture with admiration and frustration. Americans, at the beginning of their national existence, rejected the influence of England on poets and writers to create their own artistic expression. Americans are first attuned to their own culture, their own way of life, and they can proudly point to an explosive and dynamic American culture. Some Britons are beginning to feel the urge to develop within their country strong cultural nationalism to offset the influence of the great American films, books, music, theatre, and so on.

A National Point of View

A Québécois will say: Canada is one country and two nations, one French and the other English. English-speaking Canadians will reply: Canada is one country, one language; or, one country and two official languages, according to the Trudeau thesis. French Canadians will maintain that there are two nations or two societies in Canada, but members of the Parti Québécois -- a political party devoted to the secession of Quebec from the confederation -- will add: and never the twain have met, or shall meet . . .

There are 6 million French-speaking citizens in Canada and over 16 million English-speaking people, buttressed by 200 million English-speaking Americans. It is therefore easy to understand that a French writer in Canada can only reach a public of a few thousand since not all books are best sellers! An English Canadian writer has nine provinces in which to sell his book; if he americanises his stories, his books, and his language, he may even reach the American market.

French Canadians can also look to France, but France has never manifested an interest in our literature and has always remained indifferent to Quebec's culture. France looks upon our writers as poor relations, good enough to make news from time to time, especially bad political news! The famous "Vive le Quebec libre" of General de Gaulle which shook the world in 1967 did not impress Quebecers, who have learned, through history, that words and actions seldom meet on a realistic plane. Therefore, French Canadians have developed two very different cultural nationalisms. The first is oriented against the federal government to offset its taking over some aspects of our cultural life so as to inspire Quebec with a national point of view. The second, as I pointed out, is against France's "cultural domination."

It is quite difficult for our young artists and writers to refuse all the generous grants which the federal government has always bestowed on Quebec, and seek to promote a Quebec culture on their own. Without the Canadian Broadcasting Corporation, the National Film Board, the Canadian museums, the Canada Council -- all federal agencies -- French Canadian artists could not have achieved their international stature. We are aware of this cultural dichotomy, but are unable to find the means to finance our cultural expressions with and through our Quebec government. Consequently, Quebec is being accused of confining itself in a cultural ghetto, of trying in "the best of the wrong ways" to speak "internally" rather than internationally. We have developed a biased cultural nationalism, which has inspired many of our people to use a Brooklynese or a Cockney French, "le joual," as an expression of a true Quebec spirit.

What Is Joual?

It is, first, as bad a pronunciation of the word "cheval" (horse) as the American who says boyd for bird, or ain't for isn't. But it has also become a political ploy. Those francophones who believe in Canada assert that they do not speak "French" or Parisian French (which is the worst French an educated individual can speak) but an international French with a strong and charming Quebec accent.

But somehow, these parallels of pronunciation and usage within Canada's two official languages seldom interest English-speaking Canadians who pretend that French in Quebec is no good, in order not to learn it, thus forgetting that their English is no better compared with "British" English than our French is compared with "French" French. "Le joual" has become a language of the street, of the theatre, of too many films and books to demonstrate the true vitality of our national "culture Québécoise." The use of joual in Quebec is as dangerous to the dialogue we are trying to establish with other French countries, as would be the use of Brooklynese or slang to American writers if they wanted to prove their American pride or their cultural nationalism.

Our second cultural nationalism concerns French cultural domination. France could help Quebec, but its writers are mostly interested in promoting books or singers in "joual," because in doing so, their own culture stands out pure and noble, while Quebec's culture becomes an object of derision. Roger Lemelin, an illustrious French Canadian who is publisher and president of the influential La Presse (an important daily newspaper in Quebec) and a member of the Académie Goncourt in France, has warned France that to promote "le joual" is to promote the death of the French culture on this side of the ocean. For all these reasons, even for those that we ourselves have imposed on our milieu, cultural nationalism is a daily reality in Quebec.

A Daily Struggle Against Two Heads

"Un écrivain du Québec" must not only create novels, essays, or poetry good enough and sufficiently rooted in our society to capture our public, but also become sufficiently international in his outlook to lure French-speaking readers of all other French countries. As a result, he is caught in a dilemma which unfortunately tends to turn him into a frustrated artist.

Quebec writers achieve in our own province a success unmatched in English Canada. An average Canadian writer sells between three and five thousand copies whereas a Québécois novelist has every chance, if he touches a national nerve, of selling over ten thousand copies, or millions of records. A young monologuist who knows how to speak to the very heart of the Québécois held a one-man show for more than a month at Place des Arts in Montreal: over 200,000 people heard him. He does not sing or dance but offers a hilarious, sometimes tragic, monologue depicting the life, habits, politics, arts, etc., of Quebec. But if Yvon Deschamps ever wishes to present his monologue in France, he will have to use translators, and most of his humourous topics will fall on deaf French ears. His performance is vivid proof that it is possible for Quebec's artists, writers, poets, song writers, musicians, and television personalities to achieve stardom in Quebec and to become millionaires in the process. But this collective infatuation with ourselves is also a very dangerous situation because we are too withdrawn into ourselves. The American market is open to French Canadians provided they play or write in English, but by doing so they lose the very essence of their spirit. Therefore, the continental reality of North America forces them to perform in Quebec for Quebecers.

It is thus easy to understand why these two different aspects of cultural nationalism are essential in this French province.

Culture Is Political

In modern times, culture in its broad sense is available to all citizens. Ever since transistors and paperbound books have been offered at low prices, art, literature, and poetry are now easily accessible to people of all classes of society.

And because society is so extensively geared to leisure, governments must support culture with more emphasis on what we, in French, call "la culture de masse." Education, which is the sure avenue to culture, is now government-sponsored. Museums, universities, theatres, artists, all seek funds in order to be available to the public at all times, on all days, for almost every occasion. Hence, it is more and more evident that culture is political. And without a sound economy, no culture is viable in our demanding society.

Quebec has not evaded this issue. Furthermore, in order to survive the great onslaught of American and English-speaking culture, Quebec has always looked upon our cultural life with more interest than have other provincial governments because our citizens were under-educated but closely knitted together. Our society had to be helped to express its inner thoughts, aspirations, and dreams.

Without a sound economy, no culture can survive or bloom. Jean Lesage, Premier of Quebec from 1960 to 1966, father of the "révolution tranquille" which marked the awakening of French Canadians to modern times, knew that unless he could obtain more money from the federal government for reforms and culture, French Canada was doomed. At the same time, he was apprehensive of this fact: the more the federal government invested in our future, the more it would intervene in our lives. Federal control over our destiny has always met with great resistance in our province because of a built-in fear of being slowly strangled by forces stronger than our determination to remain rooted in the French fact, the French resistance, the French way of life. Cultural nationalism emerged from this convergence of federal powers over the province and its mode of life.

Culture and language are closely married, but one does not necessarily follow the other. A French Canadian trans-

planted to an English environment will not be assimilated
merely because English becomes his "langue du travail" while
French is his "langue de famille." His background, his education, his genealogy, his history have made him a citizen
entirely different from his English-speaking compatriots. A
French Canadian whose ancestors arrived in Quebec, as mine
did, in 1650 for example, can never be at home in the other
provinces. Not because he is not welcomed or has difficulties
in making new friends, but because his way of living, thinking, eating, acting, and reacting are different from those of
his new neighbours.

I believe that this is a very Latin trait in our inher-
itance. A Frenchman, born in France, and living in Toronto
or in Montreal for 20 or 35 years, still remains a Frenchman despite his familiarity with our society and our customs.

French Canadians are the same. In 1966, Quebec held
Les Etats Généraux du Canada français, a collective movement
designed to rally all French Canadians to get them to express
their ambitions and their frustrations, to inform the Quebec
government of their need for self-determination in order to
choose for themselves the kind of political system they wanted
for their children.

Les Etats Généraux helped to create the Parti Québécois
whose objective is Quebec's sovereignty. But as meetings
were held throughout Quebec and the French enclaves in other
provinces, it became clearer and clearer that a cleavage
existed between French Canadians born outside Quebec and the
Québécois, living in Quebec. French Manitobans, Ontarians,
Albertans, New Brunswickers were forced to turn to the federal
government, and they joined the other Canadians in criticiz-
ing the natural instinct of the Québécois to live amongst
themselves, for themselves only.

As a result, culture became more and more political.
Consequently, nationalism is a credo in Quebec but remains an
anathema against Quebec in other provinces and within federal
ranks. The Canadian government wants Quebec to conform, but
the Quebec government replies that Quebec is not a province
like the others.

Pulled apart by these conflicting views, many French
Canadians became Québécois even if they remained loyal to
Canada; others became Péquistes first (as members of the Parti
Québécois are known) and Québécois "à part entière" secondly.

Thus the Quebec government was also torn apart by conflicting emotions. It had to pacify some of the demands of the million voters who want Quebec to secede from Canada and use every means to achieve their goals, while it tried to appease the tensions of those who love Canada and fear the consequences of every law enacted to pacify Péquistes and reassure federalists. Law 22 proclaiming French as the official language in Quebec created turmoil in Quebec as well as outside the province. Prime Minister Trudeau went so far as to call it a political stupidity. English Quebecers felt deprived of their constitutional rights, French Québécois deplored Law 22 because it favoured English-speaking Quebecers and did not, in fact, protect "la survivance de la langue française au Québec."

Consequently, culture, which was always government controlled in Quebec, became a political issue. In these circumstances, it is easy to understand why cultural nationalism is a tool to offset the overwhelming influence on our lives of American and English literature, television, films, books, and a defensive reflex developed by long tradition of frustrations and fears.

Because the present [July 1976] Liberal government of Premier Robert Bourassa was elected with a dangerous majority, 101 out of 110 seats in the National Assembly, it must take every precaution not to appear dictatorial in its dealings with the Péquiste's official opposition. We are now faced with an increasingly explosive situation. Those French Canadians who are not tuned to the Péquiste party are not in favour of all of Bourassa's decisions. But their objections to his lack of leadership and inclination to rule by remote control have no echo. Nor can they entirely trust the leader of the opposition because they never know whether his stand against the government is anti-federalist or a peeved anti-Liberal reaction.

Once again, the opposition to Quebec's actual government is divided. Once again, cultural and political nationalism are the only refuge for all those who are frustrated with the present government, unable to give their adhesion to the Péquiste party while at the same time resenting the federal intrusion in their lives.

These are the real issues confronting Quebec. Tensions and dissensions amongst Liberals and federalists in Quebec, amongst federalists in Ottawa and federalists in Quebec, have always appeared to me to be much more dangerous than the separatist threats. The Canadian government has always been convinced that there was only one way, the federal way, to Canadian unity. Quebecers have always wondered why federal governments, Conservative or Liberal, continue to believe that federalism stems from Ottawa while all other forms of federalism are detrimental to the "national dream."

French Canadians have always known differently. It was a French Canadian, the great Henri Bourassa, who in 1917 and 1918 pushed English Canada into a positive Canadian nationalism. The federal government rejected it in favour of imperial nationalism stemming from its attachment to the British Empire.

Finally, there is another dimension of our political life which must be elucidated. The Péquiste party has been democratically founded: its militants are not underground agents or spies of the federal government. They were elected to Quebec's National Assembly through the political processes of our country. Even those who fight against the Péquiste party view dimly those who attack its members as disguised terrorists destined to destroy the foundation of our parliament.

When English Canadians point out with great emotion the fact that Quebec is essential to the very existence of Canada, few in Quebec believe in their sincerity because, as I once said publicly, if our compatriots thought we were essential to their Canadian survival, they would have informed us of our importance a bit sooner. For the first time in our history, Québécois are aware of their power to break this country or to make it. They knew who they were on this continent long before English Canadians discovered who they were, what they wanted, and where they wished to go. A feeling of belonging is inherent to the soul of every French Canadian born in Quebec, and fear for our survival becomes part of our lives as soon as we are aware of our cultural and political estrangement on this continent.

These explanations are probably too long and too short at the same time, but they form the very core of our so-called nationalism whether it is cultural, economic, or political.

Is Nationalism Detrimental To Nations?

Without nationalism, the United Nations would have remained centred around 51 nations; in 1976, it has 146 members.

Are we to pretend that each of the new countries' sense of nationalism was born out of the worldwide struggle against Nazism and fascism and the consequent founding of the United Nations? As I wrote in the beginning of this essay, countries which are imposing their strength and their laws upon smaller ones are the first to condemn the essence of nationalism they have engendered in smaller nations. Whether this nationalism is cultural or political, it rests on a desire for survival, for asserting a national personality.

Quebec is no longer an outmoded region in the world, a priest-ridden province, an uneducated land of peasants, an uncultured milieu. Our artists, writers, musicians, comedians, etc., have attained, more quickly than their English-speaking counterparts, an international stature. But as I pointed out, they too are faced with the obligation of being sufficiently national to attract a Quebec audience while being rich enough in range to please francophone audiences in the rest of the world.

English-speaking Canadian writers and comedians have the same limitations when faced with the American or the British public. Because of these two great "cultural imperialisms," English Canadians find themselves in a more difficult situation than French Canadians are vis-à-vis France. It is understandable that Toronto's writers are up in arms against the American dumping of books on the Canadian market. They have been enthusiastic in their support of the law which forced an American magazine out of the Canadian market even if the Canadian Maclean's can never replace Time.

For the first time in our common history, French and English Canadians have discovered cultural nationalism at the same time. Today, though English Canadians still view Quebec's nationalism as a threat to their concept of confederation, they are in favour of a Canadian cultural nationalism as a positive step enabling them to proclaim their Canadian identity, their Canadian independence vis-à-vis the United States or Great Britain. Quebec asserts its "Frenchness and its Québécité" for the very same reasons, toward France, Belgium, or Senegal.

To remain Canadians we must choose between a passive admiration and acceptance of all foreign countries with an English language and culture and a positive rejection of a massive import of books, films, art, television, records, etc., from these countries. When we take a positive step to assert our national identity, we are often accused of being "nationalists." Had Americans not asserted their national rights over British culture, they would not have become a great and dynamic nation able to exert their influence the world over.

French Canadians react to France's culture in exactly the same way, with the same ideals and for the same reasons. In fact, our two Canadian societies are both confronted with the same imperialism. Quebec fears France as English Canadians fear the American culture. These reactions are sane, logical, and not detrimental to good relations with France and the United States.

Cultural nationalism obliges our writers, French and English, to seek expressions more authentic with our Canadian postulates, our Canadian way of life. English-speaking Canadians may never become a cultural group important enough to influence their American neighbours; French Canadians have no hope of dominating French writers or French art; but both groups in Canada want to remain themselves because history has taught them the greatness of their country whether French or English in culture.

Cultural nationalism is the assertion of one's self. It is nothing else!

July 1976

4.

CANADIAN CULTURAL NATIONALISM
AND THE U. S. PUBLIC INTEREST

Roger Frank Swanson

Canadians have an abiding receptivity to, and fear of, cultural influences from the United States. In recent years, however, there has been increasing concern in Canada about the maintenance of an independent cultural identity in the face of massive U.S. cultural inflows. This Canadian concern extends to the influx of U.S. books, periodicals, movies, TV broadcasts, and even American professors invading Canadian universities, armed with their national and methodological loyalties. The respected Canadian Senate's Special Committee on Mass Media (the Davey Committee) could conclude in 1970 that Canada is a "cultural satellite" of the United States,[1] while the articulate Canadian Secretary of State could conclude in 1976 that Canada is doomed to "cultural oblivion" unless it takes economic control of its cultural industries.[2] Moreover, this generalized Canadian concern is not confined to the rhetorical level, for it has been accompanied by Canadian government policies which have the effect of regulating, and in some cases reducing, the U.S. cultural presence in Canada. This has major implications for U.S. private interests, as the executives of Time magazine, who maintain that they were "shabbily treated" by the Canadian government, will testify in the wake of their closing down the Canadian edition.

For U.S. government officials, Canadian cultural nationalism is an untidy phenomenon. Its internal dynamics are as difficult to define as its impact on the U.S.-Canadian relationship is difficult to assess. Indeed, U.S. officials are confronted with a rather fundamental question: Is there a U.S. public interest in Canadian cultural nationalism, and if so, how and to what extent? The thesis of this essay is that not only is Canadian cultural nationalism a legitimate area of U.S. official concern, but that it is at the same time one of the least understood and one of the most difficult issues confronting the bilateral relationship.

Canadian cultural nationalism is the least understood because it is not entirely clear whether it should be viewed as an internal Canadian matter, as a transnational nongovernmental matter affecting U.S. private interests, or as a government-to-government matter in which U.S. officials should become involved in making representations to the Canadian government. Canadian cultural nationalism is one of the most difficult areas of the U.S.-Canadian relationship both because it is so difficult to define and because it has such a great potential for mischief and misunderstanding when compared to other bilateral issues. For example, U.S.-Canadian environmental issues are always active, but they tend to be localized; strategic issues can be highly destabilizing, but they tend to be definitionally manageable; economic issues are inevitably of immense importance to both countries, but because of this, there tends to be a sense of reciprocal caution.

However, the cultural area has potential both for high drama and for destabilization because, on the Canadian side, it has such a wide potential for emotive public appeal. Far from being a passing preoccupation, Canadian cultural nationalism is grounded in a century-long quest for a national identity that defines a Canadian "separateness" from the United States. From the U.S. standpoint, the cultural area is especially amenable to misunderstanding, given those U.S. officials who see through a "first amendment optic" and recoil from any interference with the flow of information,[3] as well as those Americans who basically see Canadian cultural nationalism as either a non-tariff barrier to the free flow of goods or simply as blatant anti-Americanism.

This assessment of the U.S. public interest in Canadian cultural nationalism involves several steps, which correspond to the five sections of this essay. Part I provides a framework for dealing with the elusive concept of cultural nationalism and discusses the specific types of Canadian government policies and the cultural sectors that have been affected by these policies. Part II explores the legitimacy of U.S. government concern by placing the Canadian cultural policies in a bilateral perspective. Again, a framework is presented that delineates three conditions warranting U.S. government involvement in Canadian cultural nationalism. Having explored the Canadian and U.S. dimensions at a somewhat abstract level, the remaining sections of this essay turn to a more concrete level by examining specific cultural issues that have affected the U.S.-Canadian relationship. To date, there have been two major cultural issues of a government-to-government nature.

Part III explores the case of _Time_ magazine, which has been resolved, but in a manner contrary to U.S. interests. Part IV discusses the so-called Canadian commercial deletion/advertising case affecting U.S. broadcasting interests, which is currently [June 1976] active and highly abrasive. This case is particularly significant because evidence strongly suggests that it has resulted in a deterioration of U.S.-Canadian relations. Indeed, it is here that the question is raised: Will the U.S. government response to Canadian policies become retaliatory in nature? Part V explores the difficulties of dealing with cultural issues and those remedial steps that might be taken to alleviate some of the destabilizing impacts these issues are having on the U.S.-Canadian relationship.

I

Before discussing the U.S. public interest in Canadian cultural nationalism, there is a need for definitional clarification, and the task must begin with the phrase "cultural nationalism" itself. This phrase is a euphemism for the overall Canadian concern about the U.S. cultural impact, and, as such, is too generalized to be useful in a policy analysis. Indeed, cultural nationalism can include everything from an author complaining in 1832 about "American spelling books, dictionaries and grammar" teaching Canadian children an "anti-British dialect and idiom"[4] to Archibald MacMechan's complaint in 1920 that Canada is a "vassal state," citing as evidence "the popularity of such toys as the Teddy-bear" and "the spread by seductive advertising of the chewing gum habit."[5] Even such a confirmed internationalist as the late Prime Minister Lester B. Pearson could warn that "the threat to our national identity . . . is even greater from non-economic sources than that from economic and investment sources."[6]

Rather than try to analyze the overall phenomenon of Canadian cultural nationalism, it is useful for the purposes of this essay to discard the phrase and substitute for it the phrase "cultural retrofitting." "Retrofit" is a clumsy word but a helpful concept. Used by engineers, it means to "upgrade in place" or to improve an existing structure with new parts and equipment. For example, if applied to housing, retrofitting refers to improvements such as storm windows and insulation, whereby homeowners make their houses more energy efficient. The government itself can also become involved, given a national goal of energy conservation, by establishing tax credits for such home improvements.

In the same sense, the Canadian government has undertaken steps to improve and strengthen the Canadian cultural infrastructure with new regulations and programs. That is, Canadian cultural industries, such as broadcasting and book publishing, are upgraded with governmental assistance to insulate them against the massive cultural inflows from the United States, all in an attempt to make them more efficient and productive in furthering the Canadian goal of developing and maintaining a national identity. Cultural retrofitting is therefore defined simply as those Canadian government policies at the federal or provincial level which serve to upgrade and further a distinctive Canadian culture by encouraging a hospitable economic and social-psychological environment for its production.

Canadian cultural retrofitting, although it is primarily directed against U.S. influences, is not anti-American. Indeed, in varying degrees, all nations are engaged in cultural retrofitting, including the United States. That is, all nations are concerned to a certain extent about their cultural industries, and have developed government policies to strengthen and protect them against undue external influences. To take the United States as an example, Section 310 of the Federal Communications Act states that no foreigner can be the licensee, partner, officer, or director of any radio or television station in the United States, and foreign participation in the ownership of any such station is restricted to 20 percent. Cultural retrofitting is inherently neither positive nor negative. In Canada, for example, it can be positive in furthering Canadian unity and stability; and since a unified and stable Canada is generally regarded as being in the interests of the United States, this can be advantageous. However, cultural retrofitting can also be a negative force, at least from the U.S. standpoint, to the extent that it can disadvantageously affect U.S. private and public interests.

As cultural retrofitting refers to those Canadian government policies which strengthen a distinctive Canadian culture, it is useful to develop the concept in greater detail. Cultural retrofitting consists of two types of government action: cultural promotion and cultural protection. Although they are interrelated, the distinction between the two is important, for the type of Canadian government policy directly affects the degree to which U.S. interests may potentially be affected. In the simplest sense, cultural promotion refers to those internal policies of the Canadian government designed to reinforce and encourage the expression of Canadian culture. Cultural promotion has occurred in the areas of general culture, books, and films. The second category, cultural protection, refers to those steps taken by the Canadian government which have the effect of regulating or reducing the U.S. cultural presence in Canada. Cultural protectionism has occurred in the areas of periodicals, broadcasting, books, and professional sports. Cultural promotion policies are relatively benign as far as U.S. interests are concerned, while cultural protection policies have major implications. Having made this distinction, it is instructive to review the specific Canadian policies that are currently active in both categories.[7]

Canadian cultural promotion policies are well illustrated by the establishment of the Canada Council. The Council is an independent, partly government-funded agency, created by Parliament in 1957, to "foster and promote the study and enjoyment of, and the production of works in, the arts, humanities and social sciences," and whose program is carried out through a broad range of fellowships and grants. It is also exemplified in the book publishing industry, where federal agencies and the provincial governments of Ontario and Quebec have provided financial assistance to Canadian book publishers to help offset the high costs of production and distribution in a country with a comparatively small market and great distances. A third illustration of cultural promotion policies is in the area of films, where Canadian governments have, over the years, taken three measures to aid the development of an indigenous film industry: the establishment of the National Film Board as a Canadian production agency in 1939; the setting up of the Canadian Film Development Corporation in 1967 to provide financing for privately produced feature films; and, more recently, large tax breaks for Canadian film investors.

Cultural protectionism, it will be recalled, refers to those steps taken by the Canadian government which have the effect of regulating or reducing the U.S. cultural presence in Canada. In the periodicals industry this was evident as early as 1931 when the Bennett government imposed a short-lived (repealed in 1936) advertising tax on foreign periodicals. This was followed by the imposition of an advertising tax on the Canadian editions of foreign periodicals, introduced by the St. Laurent government in 1956 but repealed in 1958. However, in 1965 Parliament amended the Customs Act to exclude foreign periodicals containing advertising aimed at the Canadian market. It also amended the Income Tax Act to require 75 percent Canadian ownership of periodicals before advertising in them could qualify as an income tax deduction.

In March 1976, the House of Commons passed a bill requiring that any publication must be 75 percent Canadian-owned and "substantially" different (defined as 80 percent) in content from foreign publications before Canadian advertising in it can qualify as a tax-deductible business expense for a Canadian firm.

A second illustration of Canadian cultural protectionism is in the now controversial broadcasting sector. Official Canadian government involvement began in 1932, when the American National Broadcasting Company had already developed plans for a network of affiliates in Canada. The Canadian Radio Broadcasting Commission was established as the major agency for Canadian programming; in 1936 the Commission became the Canadian Broadcasting Corporation (CBC). This was followed by the Broadcast Act of 1958 which set up a Board of Broadcast Governors to control the character of Canadian programs and to encourage the use of Canadian talent. In 1968 the Canadian Radio-Television Commission (CRTC) was created to replace the Board of Broadcast Governors. In April 1975, the name was changed to Canadian Radio-Television and Telecommunications Commission, but it is still called the CRTC. Since 1968, the CRTC has regulated the form and content of broadcasting in Canada with regard to radio, television, and cable television. These regulations include specified levels of Canadian programming and advertising content and the currently disputed deletion of U.S. commercials on American programs carried on Canadian cable television. In addition, the March 1976 bill, approved by the House of Commons, also disallows income tax deductions for advertising by Canadian firms on U.S. border stations which reach the Canadian market.

A third illustration of Canadian cultural protectionism can be found in the Canadian book publishing industry. Any foreign take-overs of Canadian publishing firms now come under the jurisdiction of the screening agency established under the Foreign Investment Review Act of 1973. A final illustration is in the area of professional sports. Although Canadian governments have generally followed a policy of non-involvement, as exemplified in the cases of hockey and baseball, this has not been the case in football. In the spring of 1974, the government announced that it would take legislative action, if necessary, to bar the establishment of a Canadian-owned Toronto franchise in the now defunct World Football League because of the potential threat posed to the Canadian Football League. The threat of legislation was enough to force the owner to move the team to an American cit

II

U.S. officials would, of course, prefer that the Canadian government channel its apparently unbounded energies toward cultural promotion rather than cultural protection. Indeed, there is a temptation for U.S. officials to misread the overall phenomenon of Canadian cultural retrofitting by interpreting it as a simple case of economic protectionism. It is of course accurate to say that the thrust of Canadian cultural retrofitting is economic in nature. The economic reality of the situation is quite simply that Canadian cultural production has to compete within Canada for the attention of a Canadian audience against U.S. competition having an economic base more than fourteen times as large. That is, the "penetrating powers of U.S. culture are strongly reinforced by the economics of mass communication," whereby high U.S. expenditures for the creation and production of popular culture material can be recovered in an immense market.[8] It is because of this economic reality that the Canadian government concluded that cultural promotion is not enough, but must be accompanied by cultural protection. Indeed, from a Canadian standpoint, cultural free trade in North America is a cloak for a cultural pan–North Americanism, which means a predominance of U.S. culture in both the United States and Canada.

Canadian cultural retrofitting is therefore economic in nature, but it goes beyond the purely economic. Two distinctions can be drawn between cultural production and trade, and other economic areas. First, cultural commodities, such as television programs and magazines, are not like other commodities. For example, U.S. television programs carry rather more ethnocentric baggage than U.S. eggs or beef. That is, the content of cultural commodities reflects the behavior patterns and customs of the areas in which they are produced. To quote an Ontario Royal Commission, "Differences in societies and cultures are demonstrated in content produced, but in Canada it may disappear because of the overwhelming dominance of the American media in the content consumed."[9] A second distinction to be noted is that between product and process. For example, in the manufacturing industries, the act of producing something is often more important than the product produced, to the extent that it contributes to employment and confers other economic benefits. By contrast in the cultural industries, the product itself, whether it takes the form of books or films, is essential to national goals in furthering a sense of cultural identity and hence unity.[10]

In assessing the impact of Canadian cultural retrofitting on U.S. public interests, one must start with the premise that Canadian cultural affairs are fundamentally an internal Canadian matter. Certainly no U.S. official would be disingenuous enough to challenge the right of the Canadian government to take those steps necessary to ensure the cultural viability of Canada according to Canadian definitions. U.S. officials do have the right to assume that the Canadian government will not be indifferent to the impact on U.S. private and public interests of those actions it takes in the name of cultural retrofitting. The basic question, however, must go beyond a posturing about rights to include an assessment of the effects of these rights when implemented. In other words, the extent to which Canadian attempts at cultural retrofitting affect the U.S. public interest depends upon the nature of these policies and the manner in which they are implemented. It is naive to assume that the implementation of Canadian cultural policies, especially in the area of cultural protection, will be costless, for any such implementation affects established interests. Almost invariably, those "cultural" issues that arise from Canada are translated into hard economic issues by the time they reach Washington. It is here that a fine line must be drawn between inviolable Canadian internal matters, transnational matters affecting U.S. business interests, and legitimate government-to-government issues.

The question as to how Canadian cultural retrofitting affects the U.S. public interest is essentially a question of when the U.S. government should elevate an internal Canadian policy into a government-to-government issue by making representations to the Canadian government through the State Department. Three general conditions can be identified which would warrant such State Department involvement. These conditions are all "legitimate" in the sense that they are in accordance with general international usage. Although this usage is far from being well defined and universally accepted, the point is that these conditions are not grounded in any "special" U.S. claims involving Canada. The conditions can be most clearly expressed in the form of questions: First, is there an unacceptable degree of anti-American rhetoric by the Canadian government emanating from the process of cultural retrofitting? Second, do the Canadian government policies contravene any bilateral treaties or international agreements? Third, do these Canadian policies arbitrarily have adverse economic impacts on U.S. private interests?

In discussing these conditions individually, first, it is in the legitimate interests of the U.S. government to see that official statements of Canadian governmental policy do not unduly characterize the United States in a negative way. This is a polite way of saying that Washington might feel it necessary to protest officially to Ottawa if the Canadian government issued nasty anti-American broadsides. Notwithstanding the rhetorical creativity of Canadian ministers, the Canadian drive in cultural retrofitting is significant precisely because of the absence of an enduring anti-American polemic. This first concern is therefore relatively inactive, although there are indications that U.S. tolerance levels are not as high as they were a few years ago.

The second condition involves the U.S. insistence that Canada not contravene any bilateral treaties or international agreements in its cultural retrofitting policies. This second concern is again relatively inactive, although there are those U.S. officials who claim that certain Canadian policies have violated such agreements as the General Agreement on Tariffs and Trade (GATT). The relative inactivity of this second condition is due less to the efficiency and wisdom of Canadian governmental officials in implementing their policies than it is to the fact that Canadian cultural policies affecting the United States do not neatly fall under any bilateral treaties or international agreements.

The third and currently most active condition warranting the involvement of the State Department in Canadian cultural retrofitting concerns the even less definable area of Canadian policies arbitrarily harming U.S. private interests. This third condition differs from the second in that "arbitrary" can refer to actions of foreign governments which are not necessarily illegal, but which nonetheless discriminate against or burden U.S. commerce. The problem, of course, is to define "arbitrary" in the context of a Washington perspective, for it can include anything from the Canadian nullification of existing private contracts, to the imposition of discriminatory taxes, to the generic charge of non-national treatment of U.S. firms in Canada. Moreover, the definition of the word "arbitrary" is complicated by the multitude of government actors in Washington who are doing the defining. Indeed, this definitional problem applies to the other two conditions as well. Herein lies the difficulty in developing objective criteria of overall conditions that warrant State Department involvement in Canadian cultural retrofitting.

While it is the State Department that is primarily responsible for government-to-government dealings with Canada, other executive, regulatory, and legislative officials in

Washington, each with their own perspective and interests, are in varying degrees involved in the formulation of U.S. policy toward Canada. Moreover, there are private interest groups continually trying to influence government policies to their advantage. Washington is therefore not a homogeneous monolith but, rather, a heterogeneous collection of fiefdoms, each trying to further its interests by exercising control in its area of jurisdiction. Thus, while the State Department might take a certain position on an "international" issue, another department might take a different position, a regulatory agency such as the Federal Communications Commission might take a third position, while senators and congressmen might take an even harder line because interests of their constituency are involved.

An awareness of this decision-making process in Washington is essential in understanding the U.S. public interest in Canadian cultural retrofitting. Indeed, the case can be made that the U.S. public interest is the common denominator of what the variegated U.S. actors can agree upon in various situations. This means that there is not any objectively definable U.S. public interest except the policy outcomes of the internal U.S. bargaining process that occurs amongst governmental and private actors. It is useful to move from this rather abstract discussion of generalized conditions warranting U.S. involvement to a more concrete examination of how these conditions are active in real issues. To date there have been two major "cultural" issues at the U.S.-Canadian government-to-government level -- Time magazine, which was resolved in a manner contrary to U.S. interests; and the Canadian commercial deletion/advertising case affecting U.S. broadcasting interests, which has been highly abrasive and remains unresolved.

III

The case of Time magazine is significant on several counts. It shows how private U.S. interests based in Canada are affected by Canadian cultural retrofitting. It also illustrates how the interests of a U.S. firm can become synonymous with the national interest of the United States through the influence of that firm on the U.S. decision-making process. In addition, it demonstrates the linkage of issues (e.g., how U.S. officials "linked" a satisfactory resolution of the Time issue with other economic matters affecting the United States and Canada). Finally, it shows in an overall

sense how an issue can begin as a transnational or nongovernmental issue, then become a government-to-government issue,
after which it again becomes transnational.

The case of Time magazine has been an enduring, confusing, and destabilizing bilateral issue in the U.S.-Canadian
relationship. Culpability must be shared between both the
U.S. and the Canadian governments. The U.S. government made
Time magazine an intense government-to-government issue during the years 1956 to 1965 in a manner that considerations of
national interest did not warrant, while the Canadian government from 1970 to 1976 was clumsy in implementing its policies toward Time. Before assessing the Time case, it is useful to review its background.[11] Essentially, Time magazine
went through three periods, which reflected its mutation from
a corporation, to a symbol, to a target. The Canadian edition of Time was established in 1943; the first period, from
then until 1956, was one of becoming a successful corporate
"Canadian" citizen. Indeed, Time apparently was too successful, both because it developed a large Canadian readership
and because it, in conjunction with Reader's Digest, captured
over one-third of the total magazine advertising revenue in
Canada by 1955.

In its second period, from 1956 to 1965, Time, along
with Reader's Digest, was subjected to Canadian government
policies designed to restrict its advertising revenue. In
response to these policies, Time successfully invoked the
support of the U.S. government and thereby became a symbol of
U.S. interference in domestic Canadian affairs. Indeed, between 1956 and 1970, three separate U.S. administrations became involved in seeking to protect the positions of one or
both magazines in Canada. Both Time and Reader's Digest
strongly protested the 20 percent foreign periodical advertising tax introduced by the St. Laurent government in 1956.
In so doing, Time enlisted the support of the Eisenhower administration, with the President himself taking the unusual
step of discussing the issue directly at the summit level
with Prime Minister St. Laurent in 1956 and Prime Minister
John Diefenbaker in 1957. The Canadian tax was withdrawn in
1958. Difficulties began again for Time and Reader's Digest
in 1961 when the two magazines were specifically targeted in
the recommendations of the O'Leary Commission on Publications.
Shortly thereafter, however, the State Department warned that
the U.S. government would consider implementation of the pro-
posals as a violation of Canada's GATT obligations, with a
"senior U.S. government representative" going so far as to
threaten cancellation of a major contract for U.S. aircraft

components awarded to a Canadian firm.[12]   The U.S. ambassador to Canada presented U.S. views to the Canadian government in August 1961, and in January 1962 the issue was discussed at a meeting of the Joint U.S.-Canada Ministerial Committee on Trade and Economic Affairs.

In 1964, prior to the Pearson government's legislation of 1965, U.S. officials both publicly and privately expressed opposition to any Canadian measures which would threaten the Canadian operations of U.S. magazine publishing firms, stressing the need for trade-offs in terms of U.S. exemptions for Canada.   Both Time and the Reader's Digest were exempted from the legislation via a loophole which excluded them from the new Canadian ownership requirements.[13] The exemptions were due to successful pressures from affected interests in Canada, together with those from the U.S. government.   According to Walter Gordon, the then Canadian Minister of Finance who was responsible for the legislation, the exemption was a trade-off for the successful conclusion of the 1965 U.S.-Canada Automotive Agreement.

Time magazine entered its third and fatal period in 1970 when it became an active target of the Canadian government, unsheltered by the U.S. government.   In that year, the Davey Committee, concluding that Time and Reader's Digest posed an increasing threat to Canada's magazine industry, recommended the ending of the 1965 exemptions.   During this third period, Time was evidently sensitive to the fact that if it got the support of the U.S. government, its attempt to prove that it qualified as a "Canadian" magazine would be compromised. Time therefore fought its battle alone, keeping the State Department informed of developments.   Unlike the previous period, the U.S. government did not become actively involved.

In January 1975, the Trudeau government announced its decision to bring in legislation withdrawing the exemption and defining a Canadian magazine as one with 75 percent Canadian equity control and a "substantially" different content from foreign periodicals.   Time sought to meet the new standards, in fact, meeting the requirements regarding ownership and producing plans for a format of 41 percent Canadian content in the spring of 1975.   However, in November the government defined "substantially" different as 80 percent, and legislation was passed by the House of Commons in March 1976. Time could not meet the new standards and withdrew from internal Canadian competition.   Significantly, the Canadian government, apparently under pressure from its Quebec members, ruled that Reader's Digest stories, edited and condensed in

Canada, would count as Canadian content, regardless of their origin. Thus, for all practical purposes, the Reader's Digest exemption remains in effect.

For the current generation of U.S. governmental officials, the case of Time magazine is significant because it demonstrated that Canadian policies had less to do with culture than with who is producing it. That is, the quality and contributions of Time were not the issue, but rather, the fact that it was not a Canadian magazine. This case is therefore a "profoundly disturbing" feature for U.S. interests, to quote one U.S. official, for it illustrates to him and his colleagues the non-national treatment of U.S. corporate interests. That is, notwithstanding the fact that Time had been established in Canada for over three decades, it still had no right to be treated as a Canadian corporate citizen. In contrast, had a foreign firm been active in the United States for the same time period, and had it made the same contribution to U.S. culture during this period, it would have been accorded the rights identical to U.S. concerns.

Upon closer examination, however, it can be seen that the Time case was rather more complicated than this U.S. assessment would suggest. The non-national treatment of Time as a U.S. firm is not a legitimate U.S. government concern for two reasons. First, for almost a decade, from 1956 to 1965, Time sought, and got, the active support and involvement of the U.S. government. Second, Time's status from 1965 was grounded in an exemption by the Canadian government, which distinguished it from other foreign periodicals in Canada. In short, since 1956, Time itself gave up its right to be treated as a "typical" non-national firm in Canada because of its search for a special status, which it received. What is disturbing about the Time case is not the non-national treatment of U.S. firms, but rather, the capriciousness of the Canadian government in implementing its policies. Certainly, the impression was given that the Canadian government was "upping the ante" in dealing with Time, and that the goal of its policies was to drive Time out of Canada no matter what it did to comply with Canadian regulations. This impression was furthered by the fact that Reader's Digest ultimately received a less restrictive ruling.

In retrospect, Time magazine is a case study of how not to resolve issues. The first condition warranting U.S. government involvement was not present. There was no significant anti-American rhetoric accompanying the Canadian government measures that dealt with <u>Time</u>. Second, although at one point the State Department warned about violation of Canada's GATT obligations, the position that international agreements were being violated is not particularly convincing. Nor was there any evidence of violations of bilateral agreements in the Canadian government's actions. It is the third condition, the arbitrary and disadvantageous economic impact of Canadian policies, that seems to have been most relevant. This was particularly true during the third period when the Canadian government was incrementally defining standards for <u>Time</u>. However, even the applicability of this condition of an arbitrary implementation of Canadian policies is eroded by the fact that <u>Time</u> was operating under a special exemption, which in turn reflected the fact that the Luce publications had previously wielded much influence on the formulation of U.S. government policy. One is forced to conclude that <u>Time</u> magazine should have been regarded by the U.S. government from the beginning as a transnational rather than a government-to-government issue.

IV

The second major "cultural" issue that has arisen at the U.S.-Canadian government-to-government level involves the Canadian deletion of U.S. television commercials carried on the Canadian cable system, coupled with pending legislation disallowing as tax-deductible business expenses the costs of Canadians advertising in foreign media. This case is significant for several reasons. It shows how U.S. private interests located in the United States are affected by Canadian cultural retrofitting. It also shows how these U.S. private interests invoke support from their senators and congressmen, who in turn actively try to influence the approach and policies of the State Department.[14] Finally, it illustrates how U.S.-Canadian relations can deteriorate at the private and legislative U.S. levels while they remain "good" at the official government-to-government level.

This commercial deletion/advertising case is at the same time more complicated than the <u>Time</u> magazine case, and more disruptive. Canadian broadcasting policies affect, in principle if not in practice, some 70 U.S. television stations in 33 cities in 11 states. Such U.S. giant networks as NBC and CBS have vigorously protested the Canadian policies (the former calling them "legally and morally wrong"), as have such groups as the National Association of Broadcasters and the Motion Picture Association of America. Moreover, some 20 percent of the U.S. Senate has expressed its written concern to Secretary of State Kissinger about the Canadian policies.

The commercial deletion/advertising issue has arisen in the context of the boom in cable television in Canada, which has brought U.S. television by cable to over 40 percent of Canadian households. At the same time, however -- and this is the point at issue in the controversy -- this development has also encouraged Canadian businesses to advertise on U.S. border stations to reach Canadian viewers. The CRTC has estimated that Canadian businesses spend $20 million annually in advertising on U.S. border stations, and that an additional $30-40 million is being lost annually because U.S. multinationals can reach Canadian markets through border stations. A high proportion of this money is spent with a television station in Bellingham, Washington, serving Vancouver, British Columbia, and with New York State broadcasters in Buffalo serving the Toronto, Ontario, area.

The Canadian broadcasting policies catalyzed two centers of decision-making activity -- that of the State Department's transborder dealings with the Canadian government, and that of congressional dealings with the State Department in an attempt to influence its approach toward Canada. It is instructive to examine these centers of activity individually, beginning with the transborder dealings.[15]

The commercial deletion/advertising issue has gone through three phases at the government-to-government level. The first phase began in July 1971 with the CRTC's policy statement calling for new measures to protect the Canadian broadcasting industry. In response, affected U.S. interests sought the assistance of the State Department. The State Department instructed the U.S. embassy in Ottawa to protest an action of the CRTC which had directed certain television companies in Calgary to delete or permit the deletion of commercial messages from television programs received from outside Canada as a precondition for license renewals. On February 13, 1973, the State Department sent an aide-mémoire to the Canadian government, while also instructing relevant U.S. consular posts in Canada to report any developments in their area affecting the handling of U.S. broadcasts on Canadian CATV systems. However, notwithstanding the U.S. embassy's efforts to secure a response, the Canadian government did not reply to the U.S. protest until October 11, 1973, when the Department of External Affairs, in an aide-mémoire, rejected the suggestion that it intervene in the deletion question on grounds that the CRTC was an independent regulatory body.

The issue moved into its second phase when, on December 4, 1973, the State Department delivered a further note to the Canadian government calling attention to the increasingly widespread concern in the United States about the progressive application of the CRTC policy. The U.S. note requested a reconsideration of the policy in question. On January 16, 1974, the Canadian embassy in Washington stated that the U.S. request was under review in the interested Canadian departments and agencies; but in July, another negative response was forthcoming, this time on the basis that the matter was before the courts in Canada. (Three Buffalo television stations had filed suit in Canadian courts to test the legality of the Canadian policies.)[16] In June 1975, senior State Department officials met with border television station lawyers; there followed a Washington conference between the Federal Communications Commission Chairman, Richard Wiley, U.S. State Department officials, and the then Chairman of the CRTC, Pierre Juneau. There was no softening of the Canadian position, and in September 1975, the CRTC affirmed that its policy was appropriate and necessary. Also in September, the CRTC announced that it was making deletion of commercials from the United States by Toronto-Hamilton cable companies a precondition for license renewals. In the same month, Chairman Wiley of the FCC, after coordinating with the Department of State, held a telephone discussion with Mr. Juneau's successor, during which he tried to make clear the seriousness with which the deletion matter was being viewed in the United States. In October, several Buffalo television stations applied to the FCC for permission to erect experimental jamming mechanisms to prevent their broadcasts from being seen by Canadian viewers. In a preliminary determination the FCC subsequently advised the Buffalo stations that jamming would not violate international law but, to date, has not acted on the application. Also in October, Secretary of State Kissinger, after his Ottawa visit, said that he had discussed the television matter with the Secretary of State for External Affairs, Mr. MacEachen, that feelings in the United States were "rather intense" on the issue, but that any final disposition of the problem would have to await the decision of the Supreme Court of Canada in the suit brought by the Buffalo stations.

The issue moved into its third phase when, on January 13, 1976, a meeting between U.S. and Canadian officials was held in Ottawa. For the first time, Canadian officials agreed to consider alternatives to commercial deletion in their attempt to strengthen the Canadian television industry. However, in March, the Canadian House of Commons passed an amendment to the Income Tax Act prohibiting the deduction of television advertising expenses from business incomes for advertising on border stations beamed at the Canadian market. Since then, the issue has become even more confused. By June, although it was clear that the two governments had agreed upon the desirability of consultation, it was not clear as to precisely what they were consulting about. The U.S. position was to urge the delay of any implementation of Canadian policies while the two governments consulted in an attempt to find whether the Canadian broadcasting objectives could not just as well be met through a more positive and equitable approach. But the Canadian position was that any deferral was unlikely. In addition, the Department of External Affairs expressed concern about confusion in consultative ground rules; e.g., to what extent, if any, the consultation should go beyond the commercial deletion issue to include other broadcasting issues.

At the same time these government-to-government interactions were taking place, a second center of activity was in motion, with the U.S. Congress proceeding on a course of action all its own. By April 1974, U.S. legislative concern reached the stage where a subcommittee of the Foreign Affairs Committee of the House of Representatives held special hearings on U.S.-Canadian broadcasting relations. During these hearings, one congressman voiced his fears that those legislators concerned with Canada's commercial deletion might at some point pose a retaliatory amendment against Canada on the floor of the House, apart from the wishes of either the Foreign Affairs Committee or the State Department, "and in a moment of thoughtless nationalism we will go along. We don't like our interests intimidated either . . . ."[17]

In July 1975, a letter from fifteen U.S. senators to Secretary Kissinger complained about the Canadian attempt "to reap the benefits of U.S. television service while denying the stations who render that service any opportunity to earn the rewards of their efforts."[18] The letter concluded that "This seems to us grossly inequitable conduct by a country we have regarded as a neighbor and friend and with which this country has sought to maintain a relationship of mutual respect." The letter also challenged the State Department's transborder handling of the issue: "We think it long past time for the Department of State to take a more active role in protecting the legitimate interests of U.S. television stations." A follow-up letter was sent a month later, with four new co-signers in addition to the original fifteen, asking that they "be kept advised of exactly what courses of action" the State Department would pursue.[19]

In September 1975, Senators Warren Magnuson and Henry Jackson, both of Washington state, argued in a letter to Secretary of State Kissinger that the tax bill and commercial deletion "must be viewed as calculated trade discrimination."[20] Here it is relevant to note that Senator Magnuson is Chairman of the Senate Commerce Committee and is known to be considering retaliatory trade legislation. In October 1975, the two senators jointly sent a follow-up letter to Secretary Kissinger, stating that they were "deeply concerned that the Department of State may be, simply stated, not just reluctant but unwilling to formulate a U.S. position based on the merits of the issues in dispute."[21] Asserting that "We totally disagree with your refusal to act because 'the Department has no legal basis for objecting to the proposed amendment of Canadian tax legislation' . . .," the two senators proceeded to analyze the U.S. Trade Reform Act of 1974, making the case that the act covers advertising services as well as goods. According to this act, the President can take remedial action if he finds unfair foreign treatment of U.S. trade interests. In other words, subject to congressional approval, the President can either revoke existing trade agreement concessions or impose new duties or other restrictions on the products and services of the offending nation. Prior to the January 13, 1976, meeting in Ottawa between U.S. and Canadian officials, Senators Magnuson and Jackson sent another letter to Secretary Kissinger, expressing their concern "that the State Department is not preparing to discuss the entire range of Canadian policies adversely affecting U.S. border stations."[22]

Nor did U.S. legislative concern end with this burst of correspondence. In April 1976, a study of Canada-U.S. relations by fifteen Republican congressmen concluded in part that: "the Canadian government has charted a course in communications policy which is discriminatory to trading interests in the United States. How far Canada follows that course will ultimately determine the need for and the character of our response."[23] Three of the study's recommendations are noteworthy: first, the FCC should consider the U.S. border stations' requests for permission to "jam" their own signals toward Canada if progress is not made in negotiations; second, the U.S. Special Representative for Trade should investigate whether Canada's policies are discriminatory to U.S.

trade with Canada; and third, President Ford should undertake a similar investigation "with a view toward possible swift action under the terms of the Trade Act of 1974 if warranted."

On July 27, 1976, eighteen senators addressed a letter to the U.S. Secretary of State, expressing concern over the passage of Bill C-58, to be promulgated when the Minister of Communications decides that there is sufficient advertising time on Canadian stations to satisfy Canadian needs. The senators asked that Secretary Kissinger request immediate negotiations on the entire range of Canadian policies on border broadcasting stations before C-58 is promulgated. They recommended a "legislative response" if Canada insists on promulgating C-58, and attached to their letter a copy of a bill.[24] Their bill would empower the President, on a finding by the Federal Communications Commission that any foreign nation had treated U.S. broadcasters unfairly (C-58's provisions are defined as unfair treatment), to prohibit the importation of films, videotape recordings, and sound recordings from such nation, and to impose an excise tax of 50 percent on exports of such material to the offending country. Senator Magnuson, who was the first signer of the letter of July 27, received from the State Department a letter dated August 20, stating that it agreed with the senators that C-58 had to be considered as part of the problem. The letter was drafted before conversations between Secretary Kissinger and External Affairs Minister MacEachen, but through normal procedures was not signed by Assistant Secretary McCloskey until after the talks.

Kissinger and MacEachen met on August 17 and 18, and MacEachen was apparently very firm in refusing to allow Bill C-58 to be a matter for bilateral discussion, insisting that it was a domestic Canadian tax measure. This also becomes clear from the text of MacEachen's press conference following the talks. In the toasts given at the dinner, the broadcasting issue was not mentioned. The two men did agree that there would be talks about commercial deletion, and that these would take place in late September or early October. There is an impression in official circles that the Canadian government is anxious to negotiate a mutually satisfactory arrangement on this issue.

By January of 1977 the Canadian government took what was regarded in U.S. circles as a major conciliatory step. The Canadian cabinet recommended a moratorium for two or three years in the CRTC policy of deleting commercials from U.S. television programs brought into Canada by cable. This recommendation did not, however, alter the Canadian decision to eliminate tax deductions for Canadian advertisers using ads aimed at the Canadian market from U.S. border stations. This was, as of this writing, due to become effective within one year.

Unlike the Time magazine case, it is difficult to assess the commercial deletion/advertising issue because it remains in flux. U.S. and Canadian diplomatic positions are coalescing regarding consultative approaches; the case is pending before the Supreme Court of Canada; the Federal Communications Commission has not yet acted on the application of the Buffalo television stations to jam their own signals;[25] and the Canadian public is somewhat less than unanimous in endorsing the wisdom of these specific broadcasting policies. Nonetheless, certain assessments can be made of the issue. Of the three conditions that warrant U.S. involvement in Canadian cultural retrofitting, it can be clearly seen in this case that the policy relevance of each of the conditions depends upon the interests of the actors involved and their ability to translate these interests into governmental policy. Everyone would agree that the first condition, that of an anti-American rhetoric by the Canadian government, has not been a factor in this case. However, the second condition, that the Canadian government has contravened international agreements, is characterized by disagreement between U.S. senators and State Department officials (although there is agreement that there are no operable bilateral agreements that have been violated). Here the State Department position that there is apparently no legal basis for U.S. objections appears to be the most tenable. The case, as it now stands, is not exactly relevant under GATT, the 1934 Revision Convention for the Protection of Industrial Property, or the 1952 Geneva text of the Universal Copyright Convention.

The third condition, that of Canadian policies arbitrarily disadvantaging U.S. economic interests, seems most active in the commercial deletion/advertising case. But as has been illustrated in the foregoing examination, definitions of "arbitrary" are grounded less in an objective set of criteria than they are in the governmental bargaining process in Washington. Hence, the State Department originally became involved in the issue at the government-to-government level in response to complaints of U.S. private interests, and the Department's position has been consistently challenged by certain legislative officials who feel it is too weak in adequately representing U.S. interests. Definitions of "arbitrary" are important to the extent that they determine the type of U.S. governmental response to Canadian broadcasting policies. Will it be the State Department's definitions that prevail as it engages in consultation with the Canadian government in an effort to mesh U.S. and Canadian interests more harmoniously? Or will it be the definitions of certain U.S. legislative officials, in their attempt to catalyze retaliatory action under the 1974 U.S. trade reform legislation?

Quite apart from the future outcome of U.S. policies toward Canada on the commercial deletion/advertising issue, this case has already resulted in a deterioration of U.S.-Canadian relations. This deterioration is not occurring at the government-to-government level, but rather in the U.S. private and legislative sectors. This is an important point for Canadian policy-makers to note as they assess future costs of pursuing cultural retrofitting insofar as U.S. interests are affected. Any such assessment of possible U.S. responses to Canadian policies must go beyond the government-to-government level to include the internal U.S. private and legislative levels. The localized deterioration on the U.S. side is not occurring apart from the State Department's transborder dealings with Canada, but rather is integral to the internal dynamics upon which the State Department's approach toward Canada is based.

V

In conclusion, before discussing possible remedial solutions, it might be useful to recapitulate those points already covered. Canadian cultural retrofitting is fundamentally an internal Canadian matter, but it can have implications for U.S. interests. This is particularly the case with respect to policies of cultural protection, as opposed to cultural promotion. The question as to how these Canadian policies affect the U.S. public interest is primarily a question of when the U.S. government should elevate an internal Canadian policy into a government-to-government issue by making diplomatic representations. Three conditions have been identified which would warrant the State Department's involvement: an anti-American rhetoric by the Canadian government; Canadian contravention of existing agreements and treaties; and arbitrary treatment of U.S. private interests by the Canadian government.

Although the third condition is at the same time the most active and the most difficult to define, the policy relevance of all three conditions depends upon the decision-making process in Washington. As illustrated by the _Time_ magazine and commercial deletion/advertising cases, in the final analysis the U.S. public interest in Canadian cultural retrofitting is whatever the U.S. decision-making process, subject to its bargaining procedures, defines it to be. It is not a self-evident proposition that the policies which are the outcomes of this process will be those that best serve overall U.S. national interests. This suggests that in future attention should be directed not only at a refinement of objective criteria by which to gauge the U.S. governmental interest in Canadian cultural retrofitting, but also at an examination of those executive/legislative organizational procedures in Washington by which these criteria would be ensured a relevance to policy.

Beyond the internal U.S. decision-making dimension, there is the government-to-government dimension. A decision of the Canadian government to alter existing arrangements, quite apart from its actual implementation, creates a new and uncertain set of dynamics in which long-standing assumptions have to be reexamined on the part of affected U.S. interests. Ideally, the Canadian government should initiate government-to-government consultation at this pre-implemental stage, but if it does not, the U.S. government should do so. Consultation before implementation has the twofold advantage of allowing U.S. officials to alert the Canadian government to the potential costs and risks of pursuing a new policy direction, while it also allows Canadian officials to provide U.S. officials with assurances regarding potential negative impacts that might inhere in the new policies.

A second stage is the actual implementation of the Canadian decision to alter existing arrangements. Here again, the need for consultation, and especially negotiation, is of instrumental importance, for it can allow U.S. and Canadian officials to achieve in the most equitable manner their respective policy goals (for example, even the incremental timing of a certain policy can be of great importance in reducing negative bilateral impacts). One can avoid challenging the right of the Canadian government to devise and implement divergent policies, while at the same time insisting that it is in the interests of both Canada and the United States to maximize consultation and negotiation as a means of minimizing bilateral destabilization. Contrary to the sensitivities of certain Canadian nationalists, this neither compromises the internal integrity of the Canadian decision-making process, nor does the fact that the U.S. government alerts the Canadian government to costs in a given policy constitute a

U.S. retaliatory threat. There is, of course, another level above consultation and negotiation. This is a government-to-government confrontation, with its attendant posturing. Highly publicized confrontations can confer a certain psychic satisfaction, but they can also be as bilaterally destabilizing as they are unilaterally counterproductive.

This call for diplomatic consultation and negotiation may give the impression of belaboring the obvious. And yet, the very nature of the cultural sector as a government-to-government issue, including its highly internal and emotive Canadian content, has precluded adequate consultation and negotiation as techniques of minimizing the destabilizing bilateral impacts of Canadian policies. The commercial deletion/advertising issue provides an illustration of this. The CRTC is of course an independent regulatory agency under Canadian law, which raises the question as to when and if the Department of External Affairs should become involved, and hence the appropriateness of bilateral consultation regarding CRTC policies. For example, in reply to the February 1973 U.S. aide-mémoire, the Department of External Affairs rejected, after a frustrating eight months' delay, any suggestion that it attempt to become involved in the CRTC decision. This position appears to have been ill-advised (it was later altered), for it tended to preclude the State Department from performing its Washington brokerage role of synthesizing U.S. internal and external interests, thereby increasing the policy clout of U.S. regulatory and legislative officials. The sense of frustration at getting to the source of the problem on the part of U.S. officials was well reflected in the droll question raised by a U.S. congressman: "Are we going to be required to establish diplomatic relations with the CRTC in order to get this thing resolved?"[26]

As both the Time magazine and the commercial deletion/advertising cases illustrate, there is, for better or worse, an ad hoc quality that is necessarily built into cultural issues, a case-by-case "seat-of-the-pants" navigation. This is due to such factors as the intrinsic socioeconomic nature of cultural issues, the fact that these issues fall into that gray area where there is not an adequate international legal régime, and the fact that there are no bilateral agreements which define rules of mutually acceptable behavior. Although it is tempting to suggest joint organizations or formalized bilateral procedures as a means of resolving cultural problems, such suggestions are neither politically feasible, given the political environment in Canada, nor particularly useful, given the undefined nature of cultural issues. What one

is left with is an _ad hoc_ policy of "reciprocity." The difficulty with reciprocity is that it can be a negative as well
as a positive phenomenon, for it can include retaliation.
Hence the call of several U.S. legislators for retaliatory
action under the 1974 U.S. Trade Reform Act. Here it is important to emphasize that a key element in the U.S. response
to Canadian cultural retrofitting involves, quite simply, the
tolerance levels of U.S. executive and legislative officials.

It is therefore important that U.S. officials have an
understanding of what the Canadian government is attempting
to accomplish in its policies of cultural retrofitting. U.S.
officials need not agree with these measures, but it must be
acknowledged that the Canadian situation is dissimilar from
that of the United States and involves different cultural
needs and different types of governmental policies affecting
the private sector. In addition, it is important that U.S.
officials have a sense of equity in acknowledging those U.S.
governmental measures which are themselves restrictive concerning transborder cultural flows. For example, with regard
to book publishing, the manufacturing clause of U.S. copyright
law withholds copyright protection for books by U.S. authors
published outside of the United States. Consequently, foreign
book publishers, including Canadian firms but excluding the
British because of a special arrangement, are virtually precluded from competing in the U.S. market.

Obviously, any sense of equity on the part of U.S. officials should be shared by Canadian officials, and this applies to the rhetorical as well as the policy level. A possible illustration of a lack of equity occurred in 1970 when
the Canadian Minister of Energy, Mines and Resources delivered an address of questionable propriety on U.S. soil in
which he affirmed that "a part of the cause for the rise of
that new Canadian nationalism and determination to build
something unique, rests in the malaise that exists in your
land -- what appears to many as the sudden and tragic disap-
pearance of the American dream which, in some ways, has turned
to nightmare."[27] It is difficult to conceive of Canadian officials responding with equanimity to a U.S. official making
a comparable statement about Canada on Canadian soil.

Beyond platitudes, it is not clear what remedial actions
can be proposed regarding the destabilizing impact of Canadian cultural retrofitting on the U.S.-Canadian relationship.
Indeed, in a bilateral context, the cultural sector might
best be regarded as symptomatic of future trends in the U.S.-
Canadian relationship. Amenable neither to clear definitions

nor to definitive solutions, these problems will persist and, in all probability, increase. Given the U.S.-Canadian post-war experience of policy intimacy, it is difficult to adjust to an era in which the two countries have such highly active divergent policies. It is even more difficult to accept that the pursuit of these divergent policies is going to entail costs, and this notwithstanding calls for better understanding and more consultation and negotiation. Prescriptive remedies should therefore be correspondingly modest, and realistic, concentrating on ways of reducing miscalculation and minimizing bilateral disturbances.

For U.S. and Canadian officials, the single most useful prescription regarding the cultural sector, beyond a reflex call for more adequate consultation and negotiation, will ultimately be found in a more sophisticated awareness of the governmental and private forces active in each other's country, coupled with a better comprehension of the limited bilateral solutions available. In short, U.S. and Canadian officials are now engaged in a search for parallel interests, as opposed to the postwar preoccupation with common interests. This reflects a "comme les autres" maturity in the historical evolution of the U.S.-Canadian relationship. However, as the cultural sector illustrates, this search will not be without its perils for both nations.

July 1976

NOTES

1. *Report of the Special Senate Committee on Mass Media* (Ottawa: Queen's Printer, 1970), Vol. I, *The Uncertain Mirror*, p. 11.

2. Notes for an Address by the Honourable J. Hugh Faulkner, Secretary of State, to the Canadian-American Dialogue of the Canadian Institute for International Affairs, Winnipeg, Manitoba, May 12, 1976.

3. This "first amendment optic" is grounded in Amendment I of the U.S. Constitution which prohibits Congress from making laws "abridging the freedom of speech, or of the press."

4. Thomas Rolph, *Travelling Through Upper Canada 1832-33.*

5. Archibald MacMechan, "Canada as a Vassal State," *Canadian Historical Review*, Vol. I (December 1920), p. 350.

6. As quoted in Canada, House of Commons, *Proceedings of the Standing Committee on External Affairs and National Defence*, 28th Parliament, 2nd Session, No. 33, July 1970, p. 120.

7. This summary is based upon such useful sources as John Sloan Dickey, *Canada and the American Presence* (New York: New York University Press, 1975), especially Chapter 6, "Cultural Nationalism: Precepts and Policies," pp. 81-101; and Davidson Dunton, "The Response to Cultural Penetration," in H. Edward English, ed., *Canada-United States Relations*, Proceedings of the Academy of Political Science, Vol. 32, No. 2 (New York: 1976), pp. 63-74.

8. Dunton, *op. cit.*, p. 63.

9. The Royal Commission on Violence in the Communications Industry, *Interim Report*, Province of Ontario (Canada), January 1976, p. III-25.

10. Address by J. H. Faulkner, *op. cit.*

11. This summary is based upon interviews and on Isaiah A. Litvak and Christopher J. Maule, "Interest Group Tactics and the Politics of Foreign Investment: The *Time-Reader's Digest* Case Study," *Canadian Journal of Political Science*, Vol. VII, No. 4 (December 1974), especially pp. 617-24.

12. Ibid., p. 621.

13. Ibid., p. 619.

14. This legislative involvement goes beyond the cultural sector to include other areas of the U.S.-Canadian relationship. Indeed, one of the significant alterations in the U.S.-Canadian relationship is the increased interest and involvement of Congress as reflected in such issues as Canadian oil and natural gas exports to the United States, the Garrison Dam controversy, and Saskatchewan's nationalization of the potash industry.

15. This section is based upon interviews; U.S. House of Representatives, Foreign Affairs Committee, Subcommittee of Inter-American Affairs, Hearings on U.S.-Canadian Broadcasting Relations, April 25, 1974 (93rd Congress, 2nd Session); "U.S.-Canadian Relations," Typescript report by 15 Republican Representatives, released April 29, 1976; and Paul W. Shaw, "Purging Madison Avenue from Canadian Cable Television," Law and Policy in International Business, Vol. 7, No. 2 (Spring 1975), pp. 655-73.

16. In January of 1975 the Canadian Federal Court of Appeals ruled in favor of the CRTC and against the Buffalo stations. The Buffalo stations appealed the ruling to the Supreme Court of Canada, where the matter is pending.

17. Hearings on U.S.-Canadian Broadcasting Relations, op. cit., p. 43. The congressman said that he feared a Hickenlooper type of amendment, which on the basis of his travel to Latin America, he had found to have two consequences—it tied the State Department's hands and removed its flexibility, while it exacerbated relations between the United States and the countries involved. (The Hickenlooper Amendment to the Foreign Assistance Act of 1962 provides for the suspension of assistance to the government of any country which unjustly disadvantages U.S. private interests according to specific criteria.)

18. Letter from Senators James L. Buckley, Richard S. Schweiker, Philip A. Hart, Jacob J. Javits, Robert T. Stafford, Hugh Scott, Robert P. Griffin, J. Glenn Beall, Jr., Patrick J. Leahy, Milton R. Young, Lowell P. Weicker, Jr., Edmund S. Muskie, Quentin N. Burdick, Jesse Helms, Claiborne Pell, to the Honorable Henry A. Kissinger, Secretary of State, dated July 14, 1975.

19. Letter from Senators James L. Buckley, Lawton Chiles, Alan Cranston, Stuart Symington, and John V. Tunney, to the Honorable Henry A. Kissinger, Secretary of State, dated August 27, 1975.

20. Letter from Senators Warren G. Magnuson and Henry M. Jackson, to the Honorable Henry A. Kissinger, Secretary of State, dated September 9, 1975.

21. Letter from Senators Warren G. Magnuson and Henry M. Jackson, to the Honorable Henry A. Kissinger, Secretary of State, dated October 3, 1975.

22. Letter from Senators Warren G. Magnuson and Henry M. Jackson, to the Honorable Henry A. Kissinger, Secretary of State, dated January 6, 1976.

23. "U.S.-Canadian Relations," op. cit., Section II, p. 7.

24. Letter from Senators Warren G. Magnuson, Henry M. Jackson, John G. Tower, William E. Brock, Harrison A. Williams, Richard S. Schweiker, Patrick J. Leahy, Richard Stone, Howard Baker, Lawton Chiles, Jesse Helms, Robert T. Stafford, James B. Allen, John V. Tunney, Hugh Scott, Jacob J. Javits, James L. Buckley, and Hubert H. Humphrey, to the Honorable Henry A. Kissinger, Secretary of State, dated July 27, 1976.

25. Other possible forms of U.S. retaliation which have been mentioned include prohibiting the current practice of releasing U.S. network programs in Canada prior to their viewing in the United States, and the blacklisting by U.S. networks of Canadian television products for distribution in the United States.

26. Hearings on U.S.-Canadian Broadcasting Relations, op. cit., p. 53.

27. Text of an Address by the Honourable J. J. Greene, Minister of Energy, Mines and Resources, Canada. Delivered at the Mid-Year Meeting of the Independent Petroleum Association of America, Denver, Colorado, May 12, 1970.

PART II

IMPRESSIONS AND REFLECTIONS

The following essays relate to the proceedings of the conference. At each Pearson conference a Canadian and an American
were asked to prepare individual reports of the discussions.
The first of the two reports on the fourth Pearson conference
is by Janice L. Murray, a staff member of the Council on Foreign Relations. It is a full report of the discussions and
includes summaries of the two background papers not published
in this volume. The second report is by the late Michael
Barkway, former Editor of The Financial Times of Canada, who
died shortly after completing his essay. It is, and was intended to be, a piece in which the author dealt with major
themes of the conference rather than give a detailed account
of the proceedings.

In addition to these essays, a Canadian and an American
were asked afterwards to reflect on any aspects of the conference that were of particular interest to them. In "Choosing Our Distance," Denis Smith, Editor of Canadian Forum,
writes from the viewpoint of a deeply committed Canadian
nationalist. Roger Frank Swanson assesses the conference
particularly in light of the issues raised in his background
paper (Chapter 4 in this volume). His "Conference Reflections" include his interpretation of how the conference dealt
with some of his ideas and his own further thoughts on the
subject.

Appropriately, the final essay is by John Sloan Dickey,
President Emeritus of Dartmouth College, a long-time student

of Canadian-American relations, and the guiding spirit behind the four Pearson conferences. He offers his reflections on the role of such a series of conferences and on a subject of enduring importance -- the management of nationalism in the bilateral relationship.

5

PEARSON IV: AN AMERICAN INTERPRETATION

Janice L. Murray

This essay, roughly following the discussions at the fourth Pearson conference, attempts to include all the major points made by the various participants. In some instances, this will be somewhat repetitious of points made elsewhere in this publication; but an account which tried to avoid all repetition would be both lopsided and misleading. It should be noted at the outset that this is a personal interpretation of the proceedings; that others present would undoubtedly disagree with the writer on a number of points; and that, in any case, there were few statements and arguments made at the conference with which all the participants would agree.

*   *   *

The first session of the conference was devoted to the political context of Canadian-American relations in recent years and to an overview of the four Pearson conferences. 1968 was called a "watershed" year as a new prime minister (Trudeau) and a new president (Nixon) took office. Robert Reford has spelled out some of the implications and ensuing developments in Canadian and U.S. affairs and in the bilateral relationship in his introduction to this volume. After commenting on various ups and downs in the relationship, he concluded that at present it is tone rather than substance that seems of most concern.

John Dickey, who participated actively in all the conferences, suggested that the most conspicuous development during the five years between the first and the present conference was the continuing rise of Canadian nationalism. At several points during the first three conferences, the view was expressed that the force of nationalism had peaked;

it was proven wrong in each case. Recent events have manifested a Canadian determination to be explicit and concrete about policies to preserve and protect Canada's distinctive entity and sovereignty, and Americans are increasingly aware of this. Turning to the course of American nationalism during the same five years, it was Mr. Dickey's judgment that the Vietnam experience clearly chastened to a degree the U.S. spirit of nationalism, at least in its sense as unlimited power to lead and affect the affairs of other nations. This is reflected in the more restrained official American attitude toward certain developments in Canada, although the economic aspects of these developments are not subject to this restraint to the same degree as political matters. In general, the threat of undue arm-twisting by the United States was distinctly lessened as a result of Vietnam.

*   *   *

The first full day of discussions began with reactions to the papers by Ramsay Cook and Solange Chaput Rolland (included in this volume) and ranged over a number of topics from the historical development of cultural nationalism in Canada to ideas about the current and future force of cultural nationalism in the world at large.

In another background paper, Robert Fulford, Editor of Saturday Night, discussed developments in Canadian cultural nationalism in the last decade. Mr. Fulford argued that even in the last ten years cultural nationalism has remained a marginal force in English Canada. He suggested that English Canada is still generally internationalist in cultural matters, if one measure of this is openness to foreign ideas and cultural expression. Americans, on the other hand are much more nationalistic in this sense, since what they absorb culturally is usually American in origin. This, combined with the unselfconscious expansionism of American culture over the last fifty years, suggests that it is American nationalism which is at least one source of Canada's current problem.

Most Canadians accept the predominance of American cultural products in their lives. Nor is cultural nationalism a significant force in federal or provincial politics (with the major exception of the Parti Québécois). But there has always been a segment of the Canadian élite which has worked actively on behalf of the "Canadian identity." They create what was called "the New Nationalism" in the 1960s and is n called "cultural nationalism." Although the impulses are not new, the present wave of nationalism was probably touched off by a turning away from the United States because of its Asian policies and by increased Canadian patriotism accompanying the 1967 centennial. Simultaneously, a new generation of writers, artists, and publishers slowly attained positions of power and influence and altered the frame of reference in which national cultural issues are perceived in Canada. Thus, in the 1970s, Canadian nationalism is focusing on the central question of Canada's control of its destiny. This must necessarily be directed against the United States because of its position in and next to Canada. Canada's efforts to lessen American domination, particularly of its culture, may seem abrupt to outsiders, but they are part of the Canadian tradition.

Cultural nationalists, despite common concerns, are not united in their conception of the problem or of how it might be solved. There are two small groups: the "radicals," who are totally opposed to what the United States is and stands for; and the "melancholy conservatives," who continue their efforts to preserve Canadian nationality even though they believe that the struggle is already lost. The third group of "moderates" comprises perhaps 90 percent of those who could be called cultural nationalists. They believe that Canadian culture can and should be actively promoted. Their views are represented in the policies of the Canada Council, the Canadian Radio-Television and Telecommunications Commission (CRTC), the Department of the Secretary of State, among others.

The moderate view has been expressed in various areas in the last decade; for example:
(a) In periodical and television advertising, where the passage of Bill C-58 reinforced the general principle that Canadian advertising should support Canadian media. And, in particular, in the case of Time, Canadian cultural nationalists felt that a national news magazine should be owned and controlled by the citizens of the country in which it operates.
(b) In broadcasting, where the CRTC has insisted on increases in Canadian programming content.
(c) In films, where the federal government has supported the production of Canadian feature films (though this has not been completely successful to date).

Although Canada does not have a cultural policy as such, and because of its diversity is not likely to develop one, present policies do have certain underlying assumptions in

common, including: a healthy, accessible culture is essential to Canada's continued independent existence; state assistance is necessary because of the smallness of the market
and outside competition; there must be a Canadian as well as
an American presence in Canada's culture. There are definite indications that at least some degree of success is being achieved in various areas as a result of these cultural
policies.

The developments which began in 1967 may now be moving
into a second phase. Many who were strongly argumentative
nationalists a few years ago now find that their argument is
in many ways accepted as something to be taken into account
in the ordinary, daily round of cultural life.

*　　　　　　*　　　　　　*

Several Canadian speakers accepted the moderate nationalist viewpoint expressed by Ramsay Cook, suggesting that
the strident tone of nationalists in the 1960s has largely
disappeared, primarily because the Canadian public responds
naturally to nationalism and no longer needs that sharp goad.
The momentum of cultural nationalism has not yet fully developed, but the phenomenon is neither temporary nor frivo-
lous. It demonstrates a cultural maturity that only appears
belligerent when it comes up against established institution-
al barriers, which are now gradually being dismantled. The
process and its impulse are almost wholly domestic; Canadian
nationalists are not battling chiefly against American actions but rather against their own past immaturities.

Americans wondered if the question of what ought to be
called cultural nationalism -- which had been the subject of
considerable debate among Canadians -- really had been settled, and if, indeed, it was as generally accepted as the
Canadians implied. The conference did not really confront
the problem of defining cultural nationalism. One Canadian
participant argued that a consensus has emerged in Canada on
cultural issues, citing the general indifference in 1976 to
Time's case for retaining its privileged position, a substantial change from the public reaction of even ten years
before. Determining that a consensus exists is clearly not
the same thing as arriving at a definition, but willingness
to pursue the discussion in the absence of the latter may
have kept the conference from bogging down in an area in
which it may be impossible for any thirty people to agree.

References to the role of a small group in promoting Canadian cultural nationalism led to a number of comments on the concept and role of cultural élites. There was disagreement among Canadians present regarding the role of an élite in Canada. One defined élite as "leaders." He argued that one characteristic of the Canadian political culture is that it accepts élite leadership fairly readily, along with government involvement in culture and a collective approach to certain questions. Governments have assumed a fairly large responsibility for cultural matters in Canada from the beginning of its history. The majority of the people may not have actively demanded certain things, but they liked them once they got them. Another Canadian, however, was troubled by what he sensed as persisting American assumptions that Canada is the creation of an élite and that cultural nationalism only appeared in 1968. Americans do hear from some Canadians that cultural nationalism is an élitist concern, but, as an American pointed out, many movements are initiated and fostered by an élite and later attract a wider following. He commented on parallel movements in nineteenth-century Europe, which were generally led by cultural élites, whether they represented a majority or a minority group in a given country. For example, these élites played a significant role in the breakup of the Austro-Hungarian Empire. Some of the same phenomena, such as emphasis on preserving smaller ethnic groups, are now appearing in Canada. In general, participants were prepared to accept the term "élite" as long as it was used in the sense of a small group spearheading a larger movement and did not carry overtones of one group imposing its values and beliefs on others for its own benefit.

Differences between Canadian and American attitudes toward such matters as the role of government in culture were traced to different historical experiences. It was also suggested that part at least of Canada's difficulty in developing a cultural identity is related to its never having had a revolution. The United States did not immediately develop a unique culture after its revolution. European forms were accepted wholeheartedly at first; but they were slowly adapted to the particular American experience. Deliberate attempts were made to develop an "American" culture, but the United States never had the same type of government involvement that Canada had in the process. For one thing, Americans would tend to distrust government involvement in such matters more than Canadians do.

Another difference was that while Canada played no major role in the overall development of American culture, the

United States was very much a force in Canada's cultural development. In retrospect, a Canadian suggested, it seems that as Canada moved away from Great Britain's cultural leadership, it was not immediately ready to replace British institutions and values with uniquely Canadian ones. Thus Canada found it necessary to look to the United States for cultural leadership; until 1965 or so, there was an exaggerated dependence on the American image. This dependence did not spring suddenly into being out of nothing; it had begun to develop in the 1920s but had little visibility for some time because the British image was so predominant. But since 1965, Canada's increasing self-confidence has led to a new internal balance giving substantial place in the Canadian consciousness to Canadian artists (in the broadest sense of the term). However, another Canadian suggested that in the socioeconomic sense Canada has always been "Americanized" and that there have always been certain common aspects of North American culture, which grew out of common strands in the North American experience (opening a vast continental area, for example).

The scope of the discussion was expanded by the suggestion that a distinction can be drawn between different types of culture. An American divided "culture" into socioeconomic and political aspects, defining the latter as the way society organizes itself to deal with power. These two types of culture may be more loosely linked than is supposed. He read Mr. Cook's paper as a statement of the political theory of Canada's difference from the United States, with Mr. Cook emphasizing Canada's understanding of its distinct way of treating power. Looking at the socioeconomic side, he questioned the ultimate importance of any political culture in shaping mass culture. He doubted that the U.S. government, for example, could really do much to affect the basic socioeconomic culture of the country. He also wondered if Canadian culture would be greatly different from what it is now even if Canada were able to shut out totally American television, magazines, academic personnel, etc. The forces affecting Canadian mass culture have to do with more factors than simply government directives.

Politics can affect the so-called "high culture" in a given society, but it is much more difficult to control or direct the mass culture. All post-industrial societies may be subject to similar forces, though at different times and to differing degrees. The ability of governments in general to control and limit the effect of these forces -- the breaking down of traditional social and family bonds, transnational movements of ideas and products, shifts in occupational patterns, etc. -- at the mass level is circumscribed indeed. A further distinction was made by a Canadian within the idea of socioeconomic culture. Certain things may occur regardless of state intervention, but there is a difference between such behavioral changes and other concrete manifestations of mass culture. Virtually every country intervenes in its mass culture to a greater degree than the United States does; for example, in broadcasting. The survival of the "Quebec fact" to date is largely the result of government involvement in such areas as movies and radio.

Once the subject of Quebec was raised, the discussion would not remain confined to cultural matters. The political implications of Quebec nationalism were brought out and discussed at some length. The conference was held seven weeks prior to the election that brought the Parti Québécois to power, and although only one speaker ventured to predict a PQ victory, individuals on both delegations were deeply troubled by the possibility that Quebec might indeed separate from the rest of Canada at some point. At one extreme, it was suggested that this might not be accomplished without violence. It was said that some francophones believe that the United States would side with Quebec in such a conflict; but, in any case, if there were violence, the possibility exists that the United States would be drawn into the conflict in some fashion. However, Americans present were incredulous at the suggestion that the United States would side with a unit trying to break apart from what is regarded as the legitimate entity. They believed that officials at the policy-making and decision levels would be neutral or, at most, on the side of the anglophones. The United States would do all it could to avert Canadian fragmentation but would be forced to accept separation if it were freely arrived at through a referendum. If there were violence, the U.S. government's instinct would be to side with the established order, that is, with Ottawa. But even the remote possibility of separation and violence should make Americans think now about what their attitude in such circumstances should be. Thinking in Quebec would undoubtedly be affected by knowledge of the probable U.S. reaction. Another possibility is that such violence will not come for at least a decade. If Canada has a virulently anti-American government in the meantime, the United States might even perceive certain advantages in a balkanized Canada.

On the other hand, some Canadians (though by no means all) expressed confidence that there have been significant changes in English Canadian attitudes in recent years. That mood need not be strongly antagonistic toward, and indeed could support greater autonomy for, Quebec if English Canada comes to understand clearly that Quebec is seeking the same things in relation to the rest of Canada that English Canada is seeking in relation to the United States. Indeed, there are those, at least among a certain élite, who are coming to accept the possibility of an independent Quebec. Ottawa might not, even now, resort to violence to put down any Quebec effort at separation.

The core and crux of Quebec's problem is language, according to some. In Quebec, language and culture are often synonymous. Americanization and modernization have gone so far in Quebec (i.e., the Church is largely gone as a cultural force; the high birth rate has fallen off and population continues to decline) that language is virtually the only unifying cultural force left. No one could say whether such a "pocket of culture" could survive on its own; but the prevailing feeling was that because there are so many factors in the modern world over which governments have no control, it would be, at the least, extremely difficult for Quebec to preserve its cultural identity even if it were a sovereign state. However, the divisive forces are so strong that unless the Québécois can find a common goal and some kind of alliance around the language issue with the rest of the country, they may not be able to continue living in a unified Canada, whatever the costs of independence. The strength of the desire to be "maître chez nous" may override other, perhaps more logical, considerations.

The nature of the external American/English Canadian cultural impact on Quebec was discussed in some detail. It is difficult to state flatly that Quebec is "anti-American," because although the French Canadian élite has historically been strongly anti-American (viewing the United States as the epitome of Protestantism, materialism, and the English language), the basic impact on mass culture in Quebec has probably always come overwhelmingly from the United States. Also, René Lévesque, the new Premier of Quebec, indicated some years ago that he saw no threat to Quebec's cultural integrity in doing everything possible to attract U.S. investment to the province. But there is a strong element in Quebec that does fear American influence. They see this influence as coming via Ottawa and want to separate themselves from, essentially, "Toronto," as a symbol of much of

what they fear and dislike in the anglophone world. There
is a kind of tug-of-war in Quebec between admiration for
the United States and fear of what it represents as a threat
to Quebec's culture. Generational change, it was also noted,
is disrupting parts of the United States in much the same way
that Quebec is being affected. It is not possible for governments to erect effective barriers against the perceived
cultural changes that truly bother most people, such as loss
of respect for elders, long-haired and marijuana-smoking
youth, etc. These conflicts are part of the larger question
of what is happening to values in all post-industrial societies. During a period of rapid change, people often turn
to local institutions for protection. A relationship can be
traced between the growth, however superficial, of broader
social patterns and a simultaneous turning to smaller institutions for protection against the social and economic implications of such growth. It is necessary to ask which aspects of the problem are amenable to resolution through
public policy.

The strength of cultural nationalism and sentiment for
political separation in Quebec was viewed as having stimu-
lated regionalism throughout the rest of Canada. The problem of how far devolution could go without breaking apart
the larger entity, Canada, was of considerable concern. No
easy answers were offered to the question of when such devolution becomes irreversible. Indeed, it was argued at
one point that if Quebec separates, the rest of the country
will disintegrate, though the view was also expressed that
greater autonomy for Quebec would not necessarily weaken
English Canada's ability to exist independently alongside
the United States. Canada is seeking a form of nationalism
that will enable it to continue as a unified nation without
drowning out the various regional voices. A Canadian characterized Canada's culture as essentially regional and asserted that Ottawa could not impose a uniform culture on
every part of the country, even if it wished to do so. Explicit general discussion of Canadian regionalism ended
here, but it should be kept in mind as a continuing factor
in Canadian affairs, even though the rest of the discussions tended to group all non-francophone areas together
and discuss them as a unit.

*   *   *

In the next session, the discussants took a general,
overall look at questions of American interests in Canadian
cultural nationalism. Inevitably, this raised certain spe-

cific issues, particularly the deletion of commercials from American television programs carried into Canada, largely via Canadian cable companies, and the decision to strengthen the Canadian magazine industry through certain tax measures aimed at Time and Reader's Digest, both published in Canadian editions but owned in the United States. These issues were in the forefront of attention in the month or two preceding the conference (see pp. 72-74). The magazine issue was settled shortly before the conference, while the broadcasting problems were still very much alive.[1] In a later session, participants concentrated on these areas in greater detail (pp. 101-105). In this part of the discussion, they were cited in illustration of more general points.

The nature of the U.S. public interest in Canadian cultural nationalism was discussed by Roger Swanson in the paper published in this volume. Private American interests were outlined in a background paper by Willis Armstrong, a consultant to the U.S. Council of the International Chamber of Commerce. In dealing with the reactions of private interests to the publishing and broadcasting situations, Mr. Armstrong argued that pressure to do away with the tax exemption for businesses advertising in the Canadian editions of Time and Reader's Digest came from the Canadian publishing industry, which saw itself as the beneficiary of a diversion of advertising revenue from the two magazines. Despite all the criticism of the magazines, Canadians continued to buy and read them and presumably will keep on doing so, with only one change: Time's Canadian summary has disappeared. The real issue from the American publishers' point of view was clearly economic -- a struggle for advertising revenue -- and the struggle will remain. The publishers of Time Canada understandably considered themselves badly treated by a Canadian government which penalized them for being successful, in order to help domestic industry by distorting the terms of competition. To them, the advertising issue appears as a purely protectionist commercial measure, which has no legitimate connection with the cause of promoting indigenous Canadian culture and which in itself will not produce a profitable and successful indigenous magazine industry.

Because magazines are tangible items, they are controllable by whatever system of taxation is applied to them. The broadcasting issues, Mr. Armstrong demonstrated, are both more complex and different in principle. For one thing, governments control ownership and operating rights of telecommunications media in both countries, as they do elsewhere in the world. Private interests are involved, but they become entwined with issues of government and public interest more quickly and in a more complicated fashion than in the magazine industry, at least as that industry has operated in recent years. (Mr. Swanson discusses the nature of the broadcasting controversy in detail in his paper, pp. 68-75.)

The major private American actors that would be affected by Canadian actions in this area are, first, the Buffalo television stations, which gain about 30 percent of their total annual revenue from Canadian advertisers. The other principal actor is Station KVOS in Bellingham, Washington, which reaches most of the population of British Columbia and earns some 90 percent of its annual revenue from Canadian sources. Canada has asserted that the impetus to action, which would clearly harm these stations, is not economic but cultural (that is, it needs the funds that at present go to the United States to help develop its own television industry). It also asserts that its tax treatment of Canadian advertisers is solely a domestic question and not a matter for international consideration. The United States has recognized that Canada has the right to act as it proposes and has discussed the matter bilaterally only because the action has a direct and harmful impact on perceived American commercial interests. In the matter of deleting commercials from U.S.-broadcast programs, Canada obviously has the legal right to control its own cable companies under its law. These companies exist wholly in Canada and pay nothing for what they pick up from the airwaves. But, again, it is a matter of concern to the U.S. government because Canada's action would vitiate perceived American interests.

Mr. Armstrong also noted that there is a private Canadian interest in the broadcasting issue. There are many Canadians who like American television and who want to keep the great range of choice of programs that they now have. Knowledge of this fact has led the American television stations to speak seriously of the possibility of jamming broadcasts to Canada, in order to induce these people to speak up on their behalf. Canadian taxpayers recognize that it is better for them to have advertisers pay for television programs than to have the cost added to their taxes, through which they are already paying heavily for the CBC.

In sum, Mr. Armstrong believed that those Americans concerned about these problems feel that the continued strengthening of Canadian culture is a good cause, and one which should be served by positive measures, not by punitive action and a reduction in the freedom of choice of consumers. The possibility of confrontation in this issue area is real, because American interests have concluded that they are about to be unfairly treated by a foreign sovereign authority, which would wipe out the achievements of their private entrepreneurship without compensation, and they are not about to submit without a struggle.

*   *   *

Much of the difference in views expressed in the ensuing discussion was the result of asymmetries between the two countries. The overwhelmingly apparent, and unavoidable, asymmetry is that of size: of population, of markets, of numbers of groups and interests. This has significant consequences for attitudes on both sides of the border. Some of these differences in attitude were expressed earlier, as in the discussion of how the two nations differed in their cultural development. But while the asymmetry in size may lie at the heart of some of the disagreements between Canada and the United States in the cultural realm, it is not alone. As the preceding summary of Willis Armstrong's paper indicated, there is another element in the situation (only touched on previously), which particularly affects the American interest in Canada's cultural nationalism: the economic factor. One fundamental obstacle to bilateral understanding is that private American interests (television station owners, advertisers, magazine publishers, among others) perceive the problem under discussion as commercial in origin and try to deal with it on that basis. Canadians, on the other hand, viewed Canadian actions such as the passage of Bill C-58 and Canadian content quotas as culturally motivated. They felt that international competition -- which comes primarily from the United States and which reflects what one Canadian called the enormous vitality of American society, economy, and indeed most aspects of the American experience -- is such that Canada needs to take special economic measures for the protection and promotion of its culture.

The American participants did not, however, reflect a monolithic attitude. At one extreme, an American argued that whether or not the broadcasting question is purely commercial does not matter much ultimately. What matters is that American interests perceive it as being commercial, and this is how they will attempt to deal with it. Canadians see their actions as culturally motivated, but the same actions appear in the United States as economic protectionism. The U.S. government is not likely to deal with Canada as though the issues in question were wholly cultural, even though individuals within the government may recognize Canada's problem and feel sympathy for its goals. Another American, however, was convinced that Americans must take a broader perspective and consider if the private interests who speak up genuinely express the American national interest. He believed that the United States should have a far greater public interest in being more responsive to Canadian feelings on issues such as that involving the Bellingham TV station than in simply letting these issues work their way through the usual channels. It is usually possible in the United States to maintain a buffer between private interests and the general relationship between the two countries. He claimed that the United States is willing to accept Canada's cultural goals, an acceptance stated, or tacitly assumed, by other Americans throughout the conference.

Canadians charged that the United States has yet to go beyond rhetoric to a genuine understanding of and tolerance for Canada's cultural aspirations. One Canadian argued that America's size means that its cultural nationalism must be called cultural imperialism. Its size also means that its culture comes to others through commercial channels (films, books, television, etc.). He was thus not surprised that American businessmen do not see a difference between cultural and economic questions. The real problem arises when Canada feels compelled to take a defensive cultural reaction, by economic means, to American cultural imperialism.

The scope of the discussion was expanded by the remark that the disproportion in national size applies also to most of the countries with which the United States deals. Thus it may have to agree to treat culture as a special case in order not to pollute issues that are really more important to it. Cultural matters should be treated in a separate framework. But another American objected that because of the disproportion, the United States is expected to overlook its own interests every time a "special" issue arises. The nature of the U.S. system means that there will be opposition to giving in on these issues at a number of levels within the society. Ideally, the process of international adjustment must be facilitated; to many Americans today, however, it appears to be the United States that is doing the great part of the adjusting.

Both Americans and Canadians emphasized the need for Canada to understand the American policy process and to calculate realistically the probable U.S. response to, and the attendant costs of, any policy Canada adopts. Canadians maintained that their country does take these factors into consideration, and that their government is increasingly willing to take a tough stance against the United States when it feels this is necessary. Canada is willing to pay the costs of attaining certain cultural goals.

Americans felt that Canada is suffering from certain misperceptions. First, the strength and nature of economic clout in the American policy process is not always clear to Canadians. Second, Canadians tend to think that they need only explain their rights, assuming that if the United States knows what they are doing and why, it will accept the action. However, according to one view, the United States has never contested the Canadian right to take certain actions: it wants to concentrate instead on the implications of implementing them as they affect American interests.

Some Canadians were still mystified at the strength of the American reaction to some of their existing and proposed policies. Previous bilateral disputes have frequently been resolved relatively quietly through executive channels. Now private American actors and the U.S. Congress are getting involved to an almost unheard-of degree. Congressional perceptions are now, for apparently the first time, affecting the relationship. For instance, Canadians could understand why a Buffalo congressman would be interested in the cable television issues but could not see how a large group of senators (not all from border states) could get involved too, and why the issue had reached the foreign-ministers'-agenda level.

Americans pointed out, first, that constituents in the television case were making highly vocal demands which the government could not ignore. While the issue at stake is not important to the American GNP, it is to the people involved. They naturally become excited when they see their livelihood threatened, and the nature of their industry helps them make their complaint visible and heard.

Second, Congress has been playing an increasingly active role in Canadian-American relations in recent years. This will have major implications for the relationship. For one thing, Congress has traditionally viewed Canadian-American relations primarily in economic terms, and it is highly sensitive to economic pressures. This relates also to the warning that Canada should assess carefully the possible consequences of certain actions. The letter of July 27, 1976, signed by eighteen U.S. senators (see p. 73), raised the potential invocation of Section 301 of the 1974 Trade Act, whereby the president is empowered to take appropriate action if anyone treats American trade unfairly. How broad the implications of this section of the Trade Act are remains to be seen, as the legislation is still new. But it will doubtless be invoked by many people for many reasons, and Congress consciously included that section in the Trade Act.

In the past, the U.S. government could and did deal with Canada almost entirely through the executive branch, with little interest shown by Congress. However, a significant change has occurred. The legislative branch now has far more knowledge of and interest in various specific foreign affairs situations around the world, including Canada, and the trend seems likely to continue. It also coincides with greater public awareness of what Canada is doing that may seem injurious to the United States. At a time when issues are becoming more complex, more voices will be heard, which makes it all the harder for government representatives on both sides to deal with them. Canada was therefore urged to develop a good dialogue with Congress.

Escalation of the television issue to the point where it was discussed in the August 1976 meeting between Secretary of State Kissinger and External Affairs Minister MacEachen was attributed to the lack of more serious issues in the relationship. But an issue could not be put on the agenda unless both sides felt it belonged there. Both governments have to respond to their constituents. There are widely diverging points of view on the television issue in both countries, and when there is such divergence, things begin to escalate. Also, many complex issues are treated as simple ones in the public realm. They are capable of creating high emotions. Foreign ministers thus take them up because the symbolic quality of a minor issue may contain the grains of potential explosiveness.

An American suggested that the television issue may have reached the highest levels because it was not settled at a lower level, and it was not settled at the lower one because there were no rules for doing so. There are a variety of ways to deal with departures from the general acceptance of trade liberalization by the two nations, but as yet no rules cover the cable television situation. And because the nature of the problems is not known and clearly defined, larger numbers of people and interests will become involved, simply because they are not specifically excluded. In the absence of rules, compromise is necessary. Few specifics in the television dispute appear to reflect long-run U.S. interests; but if Canada acts as if it is confronting major American interests, it must expect the United States to react accordingly, thereby giving these interests an importance they do not really have.

In conclusion, both sides appeared ready to accept some degree of struggle before the issues at stake are resolved. Questions of process and style in problem-solving appeared more fundamental than some of the issues themselves to some participants on both delegations. Thus a Canadian commented that his government had had to do something to eliminate _Time_'s special position because it appeared to be taking so much advertising revenue (along with _Reader's Digest_), making it impossible in the circumstances to achieve a mature, healthy Canadian industry. At the same time he agreed that the style in which the government acted was not entirely satisfactory. The official point of view on both sides was stated clearly on several occasions, including those areas where each government felt it had to act in certain ways as well as those in which negotiation may be possible.

A variety of approaches to problem-solving were mentioned during the discussions. One was to try to find some general principles which both countries could abide by. No one thought that this would be simple, because the two tend to define the problem in different ways (i.e., as "trade" versus "culture"). Attempting to work through regulations was also suggested. Each country can regulate its own cultural industries, but if these regulations conflict across the border, some kind of accommodation should be sought. The United States is thus trying to find regulatory policies that will be compatible with both Canadian interests and those of the private companies. Although the latter may not be happy with the final solution, they will accept a fair decision. One American added that the United States only complained about the Canadian handling of _Time_ on the matter of Canadian content: _Time_ tried to comply with Canadian directives, but every time it did so, the Canadian content requirement was raised. This was unfair from the American point of view. The matter was handled in such a way that _Time_ could not get a definitive ruling on what policy it had to follow. He encouraged adopting a

combined technique of regulatory policies and clearly defined principles.

*   *   *

The conference then discussed a number of issue areas
that are or have been of particular concern to Canadians
in recent years, notably, the broadcasting industry (primarily television), the publishing industry, and the nationality of professors at Canadian universities.

The first speaker described the background of the
Canadian broadcasting situation in some detail.[2] The
Canadian Broadcasting Corporation (CBC) has traditionally
represented the "promotional" approach to broadcasting in
Canada, while the "protectionist" approach has been followed by the Canadian Radio-Television Commission, though
this is an oversimplification. On the whole, it could be
argued that until the era of cable television and the CRTC
arrived eight years ago, promotional policies dominated
Canadian broadcasting. The Board of Broadcast Governors,
established in 1958, wrestled with rules for Canadian content. This could be interpreted as an effort to protect
the Canadian broadcasting industry, but, in fact, it was
perceived at the time as a promotional effort.

The Canadian public was singled out as a major obstacle to using broadcasting as an instrument of cultural
nationalism. Canadian preferences for American television
and the Canadian desire for freedom of choice have made it
difficult for broadcasting initiatives to achieve the de-
sired results. Canadians were therefore warned to remember that the internal demand factor has worked against
Canada's efforts to achieve a national broadcasting policy.
The attitudes of Canadian participants at the conference
thus did not reflect what appears to be the present position of most Canadians in this area.

When cable TV became a fact, it was the Canadian demand for it that fostered its expansion in Canada. The
introduction of cable TV also brought a new economic dimension. Cable TV did not mean merely the greater penetration of American programs into Canada; American stations could carry local Canadian advertising for the area
being reached. For instance, a New York station carries
advertising aimed at the Ottawa market. Cable TV has
thus had an impact on Canadian businessmen as well as on
U.S. station operators.

At present, Canadians spend only one-third of their television viewing time watching Canadian programs, whether on Canadian or American stations. It is difficult to think of any other country where this is true, or would be tolerated. The CBC president has therefore announced a goal of persuading Canadians to watch Canadian television 50 percent of the time. Although this goal may be difficult to reach, it represents the positive, promotional side of Canadian policy. The economic implication for the Canadian public is that considerably more money must be found to go into Canadian programs. Officials want to respect people's freedom of choice, but Canada may not be able to afford to do so at this time.

As noted above, policies adopted by Canada to serve cultural ends quickly lead to economic questions for the United States. Thus Americans questioned on several grounds the Canadian plan to delete commercials (even those of Canadian advertisers aimed at Canadian markets) from American programs broadcast in Canada. It seemed to some of them a possible violation of the Helsinki agreement. Also, the logic of the plan appeared flawed. If the ultimate Canadian objective is to promote Canadian culture, it seemed odd to delete advertising while letting in American programs. Thus they suggested instead using public subsidies to develop and promote Canadian programs.

The Canadian response was that commercial deletion would serve the same purpose as, and was therefore being pursued along with, Bill C-58. The specific objective is to open up to Canadian advertisers, in Canada, the time that will eventually become available on cable systems. The ultimate intent is to keep as much advertising revenue as possible in Canada and to make it available to the Canadian media. Canadians are already spending more than half a billion dollars annually on Canadian programming. They desperately need an additional source of revenue if this sum is to be increased. Both the differences in national attitudes and an effort to compromise were indicated by the fact that the Canadian government has now agreed to discuss the methodology (that is, whether or not this is the most effective way for Canada to reach its goal), while, at the same time, the U.S. government has recognized the Canadian objective.

Other difficult questions revolve around the cable TV industry. For instance, Canadian networks sometimes buy rights to certain American programs, often at a premium,

which are also coming in on U.S. cable networks. The
Canadian network then tries to sell advertising, but it
is competing with U.S. stations which are also selling
advertising time to Canadians for the same programs. On
the American side, it was noted that the free transmission of U.S. programs has been a major factor in the
growth and prosperity of the Canadian cable industry. A
Canadian agreed that allowing the cable system to expand
runs counter to present Canadian goals and has made them
much more difficult to attain.

Many of the broader aspects of the broadcasting dispute had been raised earlier in the proceedings. In the
course of this session, more technical issues were brought
out as well. The existence of video cassettes is just beginning to pose problems. Increasing use of satellite
broadcasting may ease problems along the Canada-U.S. border but will undoubtedly raise some of the same kinds of
questions on a wider international basis. These problems
for the future were flagged, but the discussants did not
feel able to deal with their implications in detail. Pay
television is also emerging, and Canadian officials are
already wondering how to handle it. In order to reach
its goals, Canada may have to forgo the free market and
move toward a more socialist kind of controlled programming.

The possibility of jamming broadcasts from the
United States to prevent piracy of American programs has
been mentioned in a congressional report. However, a
Canadian pointed out that to be effective, the entire
border would have to be jammed -- a costly procedure for
the United States. From the American perspective, jamming appeared to serve some Canadian purposes but would
put the burden on the United States.

The same congressional report also mentioned the
possibility of recourse if U.S. interests in the broadcasting area were endangered. It said that the 1974
Trade Act could be used against a major trading partner.
This may pose a risk for Canada. This led to other
trade questions. For example, what are the possibilities that the pursuit of cultural policies may contam-
inate trade policy? Canadian businessmen have expressed
the fear that cultural policies might be used by protectionist elements in industry to justify protectionist
trade policies. On the other side, in the United States
there is at least the appearance of using the threat of

retaliation against Canadian cultural protectionism through trade policy. Third, many students of trade policy believe that government subsidy would be a sounder course to follow in the long run than trying to finance the welfare of an industry through tariff-type policies. Canada might be better served by following the subsidy approach, however difficult this might be politically.

Americans were not enthusiastic about subsidies as a technique for coping with Canada's aims in broadcasting. Several participants suggested variations on the regulatory approach to problem-solving mentioned previously. One was to combine regulatory policy with a clear Canadian statement of intent. This was done in the banking situation, and the United States then found little difficulty in accepting what Canada was doing. Second, the magnitude of the problem, and whether it will increase or decrease in the next decade, may affect whether it is worth working out regulations. Since the question of deleting advertisements seems to many Americans directly involved to be a commercial matter, the regulatory route might be best for Canada, since it would remove the issue from the commercial arena. If broadcasting issues are likely to develop along the same lines as the automobile dispute, where bilateral relations appeared threatened by potential resort to trade-reducing measures, it would be better to seek a reasonable alternative than to deal with issues on a piecemeal basis.

The participants did not attempt to reach agreement or even to compromise on any of these issues. However, at the end of this session, a Canadian commented on several themes in the discussion that appeared of particular significance from the Canadian perspective. The broadcasting controversy, he believed, is a forerunner of issues that will preoccupy people on both sides of the border in the next ten years. The disparity of size and Canada's vulnerability and determination to maintain independence as a nation-state mean that the issues will not go away. If Canada were entirely hard-nosed on the subject of cultural nationalism, it would jam the border itself. It would be unfortunate for the United States if Canada took such a stance, but Canada does not intend to go that route. The access of Canadians to ideas from beyond their borders is on balance a good thing. Thus Canada's answer to the dilemma must be a complex one. It cannot take a totally isolationist approach; even if this were feasible, it would not be desirable. Canada must find a way to keep its doors open to the free flow of ideas while assuring its indigenous development. Finally, he felt that both countries will have to deal with questions on an area-by-area basis, accepting the necessity of compromise.

*　　　　　*　　　　　*

The problems Canada faces in the book publishing industry were illustrated in a study done for the Canadian government in 1969, which showed that two-thirds of the books read in Canada (by value) were imports, and that 80 percent of the imports came from the United States. This has changed somewhat, but Canadian publishers still have considerably less than half of the Canadian market.

Canadians reported a growing feeling in Canada that its share of the market is too small and that there should be a drive toward increasing the internal production and consumption of Canadian books. Thus far Canada has pursued a cultural promotion route toward this goal. Regulation presents problems because it would require negotiating with individual provinces. But if Canada is successful, by whatever method, the flow of American books to Canada will be displaced and reduced to a certain degree. Canada is now taking the first steps to introduce measures leading toward Canadian ownership of the publishing industry in Canada. Measures may have to be taken eventually that will be drastic as far as the position of American publishers in Canada is concerned.

Intra-governmental issues are not involved at the moment, but this may change. When Canadian publishers look at the Canadian market, they find that Americans have already taken more than half of it. The Canadian publishers feel that they need government support to secure their own market because, in contrast to U.S. publishers that are subsidiaries of larger companies, their credit position is generally not as strong. Thus Canadian publishers may exert pressure on their government for support in three or four years, when they have mobilized their case.

On the whole, Americans at the conference did not question the Canadian view of the situation, or what Canada might do in the future. However, a potential irritant was identified. American books exported to Canada represent about 60 percent of total U.S. book exports, and American publishers are highly aggressive where their export markets are concerned. If they feel threatened they may well seek support from their own government.

One major problem from the viewpoint of cultural
nationalism is that American publishers in Canada are interested primarily in selling textbooks and secondly in
distributing American, not Canadian, books. The lack of
Canadian social science textbooks written for Canadian
students (due partly at least to Canadian slowness in becoming active in the social sciences) was a matter of concern to Canadians at the conference. For example, there
is an American text on international organizations for $9,
while a Canadian text on the same subject costs $31. The
U.S. book is used because it is so much cheaper, but it
does not provide a Canadian perspective on international
organizations. On occasion, American economic textbooks
have been adapted somewhat by someone in Canada for Canadian use. This might be a partial solution to the problem,
although probably not at the university level. In general,
the problem of assuring Canadian content appeared more serious at the primary and secondary levels. An American suggested that in some areas where the national perspective
does not matter, such as mathematics, Canadians reap cost-
saving benefits because of their involvement in the larger
U.S. mass market. However, it is textbooks that provide the
profits for publishing houses. If Canadian publishers do not
have the Canadian textbook market, their financial condition
is so tight that they cannot produce other types of books.

*   *   *

There was some discussion of the issue of nationality
of professors at Canadian universities. The question did
not arise ten years ago, even with regard to sensitive
political science jobs. Indeed, in the early 1960s, the
United States produced more Ph.D.s than it needed, and the
surplus met Canada's need at the time. This followed a
Canadian tradition, dating from the nineteenth century, of
importing foreign professors. With the great university
expansion of the 1950s and 1960s, there was a sudden, large-
scale need for faculty, which Canada could not then have met
from its own resources.

The issue of nationality is now overtly discussed.
Some of the Canadians present felt that it is no longer a
problem, partly because it is now out in the open and partly because of a stable undergraduate population, which
means that university hiring will be at a virtual halt for
the next ten to twenty years. It was noted, however, that
nationality is a political issue in Ontario. The Ontario
legislature has had a committee on nationalism, which took

a virulent tone regarding the nationality of academic personnel in the province. The Ministry of Education has demanded that universities improve the situation, at least in hiring new people.

It was also suggested that focusing on questions of citizenship was in some ways a red herring. The problem is not that Americans per se are teaching in Canadian universities but rather that, whether they take Canadian citizenship or not, they retain and therefore tend to pass on their original training and ideas. This is particularly important in the social sciences. Thus, in the 1960s, Canadian universities were drawn into the struggle between quantitative and traditional American social scientists, with faculties being torn apart. As far as Canada was concerned, the real cultural imperialists then were the anti-American Americans teaching in Canada who were totally uninterested in Canada.

Americans commented that Americans teaching in Canada have reported that they have to walk very gingerly around the nationality question and that there is more antagonism about it than appeared in the discussion. However, a Canadian concluded that there is no monolithic Canadian attitude toward the problem of American academics in Canadian universities, although there is a good deal of discussion about it. He had known Americans who felt quite free to raise the issues mentioned in a Canadian setting, and he believed that Canada had preserved a sense of academic freedom.

*   *   *

In the last session of the conference -- following the practice of earlier Pearson conferences -- the participants looked again at some of the issues raised during the conference, commenting on them in the framework of the overall relationship between Canada and the United States.

Mr. Reford observed that he now felt somewhat less concerned about the "tone" of the relationship than he had at the outset. Despite the emotional nature of cultural issues, people at the conference had been able to discuss them calmly. Also, mutual awareness and dialogue appear to be taking place at inter-governmental levels. However, he did not take these signs to mean that there are no real problems left. Future issues were suggested, especially those arising from new technologies. In addition, there remains the question of who will handle present and future problems: should economic departments of governments deal with cultural dilemmas?

An American thought that the problem of disparity in size, both between the two countries and in terms of the absolute volume of everything that could be called culture coming out of the United States, was less emphasized at the conference than it might have been. This disproportion creates a dilemma for Canadians. If they want to be part of the world culture as well as have their own, they must live with the fact that a disproportionate part of the world culture comes from the United States. Each individual can take in the total "culture" to which he is exposed without depriving anyone else of it. While each person makes his own choice, and although this choice is affected by national factors, any Canadian's culture is bound to have in it more things of American origin than an American's would have of Canadian origin. Thus Canada's problems stem more from the fact that culture is imported that that it is consciously exported. Much of what is now seen as a problem was in the past simply the satisfying of Canadian desires for things that could only come from the United States. This is now changing, as Canadians seek to ensure that the Canadian alternative will not disappear, but the decisions this entails will be extremely complex. The process of change is always difficult to accommodate, economically, politically, and socially.

Cultural issues do give rise to economic questions. Although there is no American policy -- or interest -- in pushing American cultural penetration of Canada, there are American commercial interests in selling culture to Canada, comparable to those in selling goods. But the law of comparative advantage, which says that under free trade Canada will always be able to do what it does best, clearly does not apply to cultural activities that need to be supported by a market, and gives no guarantee of diversity, which may be essential in culture whereas it is not in economics. Because of the asymmetry, Canada may well have to do more things than the United States should be allowed to do (including some element of protection) in order to foster Canadian culture.

The conference touched on these questions in considering whether cultural issues could be handled -- bilaterally or multilaterally -- according to a certain set of principles, or whether they must be dealt with on an ad hoc basis as they arise, which would almost always mean bilaterally. The latter course is risky, although if we could be certain that some problems would eventually become self-regulating we could avoid looking for principles in those areas. For instance, the conference felt that this has happened already in the matter of university professors.

Finally, although the conference dealt with these issues in the Canadian-American context, they are part of a more general phenomenon. Nation-states may not always be the relevant framework for handling certain issues, but the problems and costs of interdependence must also be considered. The idea of "selective de-linking" of a country from international interdependencies offers a way to look at culture and cultural nationalism in the larger context, although the problem of size between unequal entities remains unavoidable. If problems of cultural relations exist on a wider scale than North America, perhaps something can be done about them at a more general level. A code of permitted practices might be designed as an exception to the GATT's ordinary rules. In the Canadian-American context, this might mean seeking agreement on activities where cultural considerations should dominate, even if this requires economic protectionism. Economic and trade rules governing other activities should be modified sufficiently to do some good for Canadian culture while being reasonably fair to purely commercial interests in the United States. All this could be done asymmetrically so that there are no loopholes permitting a great deal of American protectionism and the chances for Canadian culture to have an impact on Americans are not reduced. Finally, there should be a way to keep the access to American culture that many Canadians appear to want and to prevent the undesirable effects of creating a hothouse climate in Canada. All this sounds in some ways like a case for a set of rules that would modify the norms of economic cooperation and liberalization, in rather special ways.

Some Americans returned during this session to an issue that had concerned them throughout the conference: they argued again that Canada must define clearly what it wants in the various cultural areas under discussion. This led to questions of the nature of government involvement in the issues. Americans recognized that there may be debate on certain issues in each country, but they wanted governments to become involved only when true inter-governmental issues arise. One maintained that officials on both sides generally do make sincere efforts to understand their differences. He looked at the difference in size and weight between the two countries in an official context, arguing that it does not affect official relations and urging Canadians to rid themselves of their obsession with size.

The fundamental difference in attitude toward the size differential, at least among participants in this conference, was made clear in the ensuing exchange. The Canadian view was that although Canada may suffer no prejudice because of its size in official dealings, its concern with the problem is still legitimate. In broadcasting, size _is_ the issue. The problem will not go away, and it is the driving force behind Canadian policy in this case as in others. However, a Canadian admitted that it is difficult to deal with problems created by the size disparity because the majority of Canadians are still indifferent to it. There is no self-denying ethic in Canada with regard to the consumption of U.S. culture. Solutions alluded to during the conference, such as licensing cable companies to carry only Canadian programs, therefore will not be acceptable to most Canadians. Americans understood Canada's feelings about its size in relation to the United States, but one pointed out that, from the American perspective, Canada appears as one of the six or seven top economic powers in the world, by any index. It has one of the world's better diplomatic services and an important, independent international role. It is only the accident of geography that makes Canadians underestimate themselves and their position. Indeed, he went on to suggest, it is the peculiar set of circumstances in North America that gives all its inhabitants a different approach to cultural matters. The "expressionist culture" that both countries are trying to find their way through is quite different from what they inherited from Europe.

As suggested above, the particular mix of people at the conference resulted in a somewhat skewed picture of the overall situation. One Canadian thought that if a number of other actors had been present, the group would have been left feeling less comfortable about the tone of the relationship. There are still those, for instance, who are unhappy with the _Time_ decision. Representatives of radio interests also would have left the group feeling less sanguine. The best understanding between the two countries often comes at the State/External Affairs level. This may be illuminating but should not be overly reassuring. Actors in controversies may understand each other, but they will compromise only when forced to. Politicians are affected by the actors directly involved, by broad public attitudes, and by their own understanding of the issues. They are also affected by their appreciation of the relative importance of issues to themselves. This makes it particularly important to understand the impact of politicians and legislators on disputes over cultural nationalism.

The role of persuasion was identified as a major difference between the two systems. A Canadian stated that it is impossible to act in the United States without persuading the various interests involved, whereas it has been possible in Canada. This is changing, and Canadians now need to pursue the persuasive elaboration of policy, both for themselves and for the United States, especially in cases where the latter will be affected. Looking at the Time decision in this context, one sees that the Senate report emphasized the importance of being orderly and explicit in dealing with the situation. Some members of Parliament became unhappy during the final stages of the debate, not with the objective of Bill C-58 but with the disorderly way in which the 80 percent content rule was introduced. They felt that this was not good either for the government or for orderly relations with the United States. Another Canadian added that some decisions, including that on Time and Reader's Digest, reflect regional differences. He thought this difference between the two countries was illustrated by the fact that it was a Canadian who had put the case for continuing the ad hoc approach to problem-solving, while an American argued for a generalized approach.

A Canadian had perceived from the conference that Canada is much more aware than the United States is of the government's role in cultural issues. He wondered why Canada has been able to find a balance of payments in trade but cannot seem to reach a similar balance in cultural exchanges. Canada, he believed, is heading toward the development of cultural policies by becoming more state-interventionist and wondered if it might be possible instead to develop market forces in Canada in conjunction with the Americans. Canada's size prevents its market forces from doing the task alone. The United States helped Canada develop its industrial resources, and a similar arrangement may be possible in the cultural field. Otherwise, he could foresee only an increase in state intervention.

The last speakers returned to the problem of finding ways of dealing with the issues. A Canadian noted the tendency, remarked on by various speakers, for U.S. interests to take an economic interpretation of Canadian cultural concerns. He wondered if a series of conferences similar to this one could offer a way to help the various parties involved understand one another. An American added that he had been thinking about the possibility of a joint commission on North American cultural affairs. It would have no particular power but could begin to discuss, on a broad basis, cultural and economic aspects of the problem. Another possibility would be to set up a commission of distinguished citizens from both countries to consider the questions, perhaps including some Europeans to gain the benefit of their experience with transborder cultural issues. This would also encourage systematic examination of the questions; the present tendency is to deal with individual episodes as they arise. A Canadian commented that although he was on the whole opposed to institutions as a way of dealing with bilateral relations, he did think it worthwhile to see if the methods of the International Joint Commission could be applied in other areas. Thus one would begin by talking to technicians and then make recommendations to the two governments. As Canadians look at the history of institutions, they tend to see them as deliberate gestures toward continentalism on Canada's part, but these institutions in fact usually developed in response to the Canadian government's desire to control and defend its interests.

It was symbolic of the Pearson conferences as a whole that this fourth one ended not with any attempt to make one point of view prevail but rather with the recognition of significant differences between Canada and the United States and an effort to think imaginatively about how to conduct bilateral relations in the presence of such differences.

April 1977

NOTES

1. The tax exemption was removed from _Time_ but not from _Reader's Digest_, for a variety of reasons.

2. Because of the language difference, Quebec faces less of a problem than the rest of Canada in this area. Broadcasting is heavily subsidized in Quebec. In order to reach the Quebec market, American programs must be dubbed. There has been an increase in recent years in U.S. efforts to dub programs, and advertising is sold for these; but it is still a marginal issue in Quebec as a whole.

6.

CHOOSING OUR DISTANCE

Denis Smith

The Niagara conference on Canadian cultural nationalism and
Canadian-American relations came at a time of pause when
reflection was possible and appropriate. By September 1976
the activity of the federal government in developing a cultural policy seemed to have concluded; and the 1976 Quebec
election, with all its cultural implications, was still two
months away.

On the eve of the conference the Canadian government
brought into force Bill C-58 concerning tax exemptions for
advertising expenditures, which meant that, while the American delegates retained a lively curiosity about the intent of
the legislation and the degree of support for it, the prolonged affair had finally passed into history and was no
longer regarded as a subject of current grievance. It was,
however, in the air throughout the discussions as the most
immediate instance of Canadian-American disagreement and a
possible harbinger of disputes to come.

For about six months before the conference -- or since
the beginning of 1976 -- a notable change in the cultural
climate of English-speaking Canada had been evident. The
period of intense and often strident pressure from a nationalist minority for tangible measures of cultural support from
the federal government, maintained in a popular atmosphere of
indifference or contempt for such measures, had given way to
a more relaxed period of fresh consensus in which the nationalist case seemed to have gained fairly general public
acceptance. That gradual change of atmosphere was exemplified by the federal government's decision, announced in
January 1975, to tackle the anomaly of the special tax pri-
vileges granted to advertisers in the Canadian editions of
Time and Reader's Digest and on border American television
stations whose signals are available in Canadian metropolitan

centres. (The Liberal cabinet of Pierre Elliott Trudeau, although it contained several moderately nationalist English-speaking members, had always been predominantly anti-nationalist. In this stance it reflected the powerful conviction of the Prime Minister. The decision to proceed with such nationalist legislation, of substantial commercial import, could only mean that the cabinet majority had conceded reluctantly to its perception of a significant change in public sentiment.)

A second sign of the changing orthodoxy was the Canadian Broadcasting Corporation's production, in the spring of 1976, of a major six-hour series on The Great Canadian Culture Hunt, which was as much advocacy as it was reporting. It gained large prime-time audiences and favorable reviews. By May 1976 when Susan Crean published her account of the English-speaking Canadian cultural quest, Who's Afraid of Canadian Culture?, one of the recurrent themes in the (mostly anti-nationalist) reviews was, ironically, that her story of cultural deprivation and exclusion from the domestic market was already passé. The judgment was wrong but its existence was symptomatic: Critics of nationalist measures in support of the arts could no longer simply reject the nationalist case and expect a sympathetic response from their audiences. They had to concede much of the case and seek to undermine it with more subtlety. Finally there was the publication in the late spring of 1976 of the first two volumes of the Symons report on Canadian Studies,[1] which catalogued the extent of recent scholarly neglect of Canada. The report was greeted with almost universal support in newspaper features and editorials.

So, by the time of the conference, if the circumstances of Canadian cultural institutions were still frequently precarious, there seemed to be wide public understanding of their plight and recognition that many of their difficulties stem from Canada's openness to American cultural influences. This did not mean that there were obvious and widely accepted policies to meet those difficulties (that is a matter of leadership still to come); it did mean that the institutions and their spokesmen no longer felt isolated from and antagonistic to common sentiment, as they usually had in the late 1960s and early 1970s.

The change of cultural atmosphere in English-speaking Canada was signified most vividly at the conference by two examples which would, I think, have been inconceivable five years ago. One was the fact that Ramsay Cook's account of Canadian cultural nationalism was stated moderately and posi-

tively in terms that were acceptable to the Canadian nationalists present. For Mr. Cook, the Liberal anti-nationalist
historian, Canadian cultural nationalism had passed out of
the realm of tendentious sectarianism into that of indisput-
able and perhaps inevitable historical fact. Things must
have come a long way for that.

The second striking example was the forceful and un-
apologetic nationalism of two Canadian civil servants, members of the conference, one from the Secretary of State's
Department and one from the Department of External Affairs.
Their confident assertion of what they saw as the Canadian
interest in cultural affairs, and their willingness to contemplate actions which were bound to ruffle American feath-
ers, were revelations, I think, to most of the delegates.
Something approaching a revolution in consciousness must
certainly have occurred in Ottawa to produce bureaucrats so
much at odds with the postwar orthodoxies and so free to
express their thoughts in public. One of them, the Under
Secretary of State, André Fortier, more recently repeated
some of his remarks publicly in Washington at the Symposium
on 20th Century Canadian Culture. "The main effect of all
this government intervention," he said, speaking of the
recent record of cultural support from Ottawa, "has been to
assure a place on the shelf for Canadian cultural products."

At its heart, are the notions of choice and access,
the opportunity for Canadian artists to live, work
and attain a modicum of critical and financial success in Canada, and the opportunity for Canadians to-
experience their work. All of these measures have
been good; indeed necessary to survival. I think
they are inadequate for growth and self-fulfill-
ment. . . .

The fact remains that our national self-aware-
ness is still threatened; our cultural delivery
systems, if I may be permitted so prosaic a phrase,
are so full of foreign products that there is scarce-
ly room for the homegrown variety. Our problem is
what to do about it. . . .

We know. . .that whatever mechanisms are employed we will be up against strong economic forces
that have traditionally worked to our disadvantage --
the ready availability of cheap attractive foreign
products and the tremendous expense of producing our
own and making them available. Ought the government

> to intervene more strongly in the production and
> distribution of Canadian products to ensure that
> its citizens do indeed have a cultural choice?
> Or should the government leave this field of acti-
> vity largely to independent entrepreneurs? Or is
> there a middle ground where the government would
> focus on indirect support through legislation and
> regulation to offset the competitive disadvantage
> facing Canadians in this area, a disadvantage that
> is built into the existing market structure?[2]

The "middle ground" previously occupied by the Canadian government in the arts has been the ground of direct subsidy through the Canada Council: a policy which has staved off bankruptcy for many institutions but which has neglected the structure of the cultural market that often prevents those institutions from reaching their primary domestic audience. André Fortier's recognition of a new middle ground of legislative interference in the market is not a statement of government policy, but it confirms the shift in national consensus about the arts in Canada, and probably foreshadows more active government intervention in their support in future. His position confirms the sense expressed by most Canadian participants in the conference that cultural nationalism has now come into the mainstream of political discussion in English-speaking Canada, but has not yet reached its peak. Its evolution was seen as part of the normal growth of national identity. As a number of persons said, there are obvious parallels between the contemporary flowering of the arts and national self-consciousness in English-speaking Canada, the earlier creative blossoming of Quebec in the 1960s, and the development of an indigenous American culture in the nineteenth century as European forms and standards were gradually sloughed off for national ones.

The ways in which Canadians perceive the role of government were much remarked upon. Several Canadians emphasized their view that government must play a central role in the stimulation of both artists and their audiences in Canada. The conviction appeared to be an article of faith arousing little anxiety among Canadians familiar with the formative influences of the National Film Board, the Canadian Broadcasting Corporation (CBC), the National Gallery, the Canada Council, Artbank, and the Canadian Radio-Television and Telecommunications Commission (CRTC). This assumption about government activity may have appeared eccentric to some of the American delegates more accustomed to the dominance of market values in the American cultural industries. (It was at least made clear that when Canadian cultural policies have an adverse effect upon the profits of American companies -- as in the case of Canadian regulation of advertising on border television stations -- the American reaction is likely to reflect commercial interest rather than cultural sensitivity.)

American participants did note the readiness of the American government to intervene in its own market to protect it by regulation for the support of American entrepreneurs. They could therefore respect, in principle, the right of the Canadian government to do likewise, provided the rules were made clear; but that theoretical respect was unlikely to temper American efforts to defend established American interests in the Canadian market, to emphasize their commercial nature, and to ignore their cultural implications. The Canadians were left with the common-sense view (but one that is relatively novel in a country only slowly discarding its colonial assumptions) that the Canadian interest must be defined and asserted by Canadians.

A distinction was drawn by an American between high culture, which is susceptible to élite management because it is <u>directed</u> only to the élite, and mass culture. He suggested that the extensions of Canadian cultural policy now being considered were efforts to influence mass culture, which is shaped by forces common to all post-industrial societies, and probably beyond the influence of élitist regulation. Aside from noting that this is a real possibility, but asserting that Canadian policy would be aimed at encouraging local control, public choice, and marginal rather than central changes in popular habits, the conference neglected to take up this complicating point in detail. It is one that the CRTC and the CBC struggle with daily in a mood of increasing pessimism; and it is related to the rapid advance of technology which brings us cable and satellite transmission just as we have shakily established the machinery of licensing and control over conventional television broadcasting. It concerns fundamental questions of political versus economic and cultural determinism which were not touched upon explicitly at the conference. The implicit assumption of the Canadian delegates seemed to be that a community's political will (if it chooses to exercise that will) can substantially determine its cultural atmosphere at all levels, to some considerable extent in defiance of strong social and economic forces. The concept of mass society is, further, an American one which fits peculiarly American circumstances; it may be that Canada is not a mass society, except in the features extending into it from American mass society, and therefore susceptible to shrewd national cultural leadership. (It also seems questionable even to claim for American society that mass culture is beyond the influence of leadership or "élitist" manipulation.)

While most of the delegates' attention was devoted to the cultural policies of the Canadian government as they reflect English-speaking pressures and interests, Ottawa's embarrassments over bilingual air traffic control and the signs of growing support for the Parti Québécois inevitably led the meeting to discuss the Quebec independence movement and its consequences for Canadian-American relations. The discussion, which focused on the potential attitude of the United States government to an independent Quebec, was not strictly within the subject of the conference, but the independence movement's potential for disturbing habit and convention was great enough that the matter could not be ignored. The American response was a proper diplomatic one, that the United States government recognizes established governments and does not interfere in domestic politics. There discussion stopped. One could speculate that the State Department's attitude to the independence movement is in fact more complicated than this, and that many considerations of American national interest enter into the calculation, not all of them constant in all circumstances. The pro forma reassurance about American support for the status quo was not perhaps as reassuring as it appeared to be -- since tomorrow's status quo may not be today's.

One point which was stated but not sufficiently emphasized was that cultural nationalists in English-speaking Canada in the 1970s are not antagonists of Quebec nationalism, but generally its supporters. Quebec's awakening has been regarded increasingly in the English-speaking cultural community as an example and inspiration rather than as a threat. What is seen from outside the country as cultural division and disintegration can instead be seen from within as a shared (or at least parallel) search for independence by two colonized communities. It is not quite axiomatic that a victory for the independence movement in Quebec must be a defeat for Canada; it is just conceivable that the two nationalist movements could develop together in a way which would reinforce the confidence and will to survive of both communities.

That is not yet the official view in Ottawa, or the dominant view in the country; but as the need to deal peace-

fully and realistically with the fact of Quebec nationalism
becomes more pressing, the paradox may be recognized in both
communities as a creative one. Such recognition might encourage more activist cultural policies in both Ottawa and
Quebec City, which would challenge American interests across
the whole range of the cultural industries. According to
this analysis, the narrow American interest would thus lie
clearly in undermining Quebec nationalism because that action
would assist a Canadian federal government, which is anti-
nationalist on principle and complacent about the continuing
dominance of American cultural and economic influences in
Canada. (Perhaps the warm congressional response to Prime
Minister Trudeau's promise of continuing Canadian unity
revealed Washington's intuition that the American link with
Canada inverts the classical maxim, divide and rule.)

For most of the conference, the American participants
seemed to be fascinated observers at yet another Canadian
session of encounter therapy, genuinely tolerant, and concerned in a good-neighbourly way about the (genially hypo-
chondriac?) patient's well-being. I sensed occasionally that
it is difficult for some Americans (as it is for Canadians)
to believe that Canada may have interests and a destiny
different in important ways from those of the United States.
For thirty years Canada has given the United States no reason
to think its interests and destiny are separate, so the
difficulty is understandable. But the existence of a new
Canadian mood was manifest, and I believe that on both sides
the meeting reflected a growing willingness to accept the
consequences of that change. This does not guarantee easy
relations, but it does suggest that both countries may pursue
their national interests in ways that will maintain a high
level of mutual respect and civility. The forthcoming initiatives in cultural relations, however, are almost certain
to come from Ottawa -- or Quebec City -- rather than Washington.

April 1977

NOTES

1. T. H. B. Symons, "To Know Ourselves: The Report of the Commission on Canadian Studies" (Ottawa: Association of Universities and Colleges of Canada, 1976).

2. "The Role of Government in the Development of Culture and the Arts in Canada," a speech by André Fortier, Under Secretary of State, at the 20th Century Canadian Culture Symposium, Washington, D.C., March 23, 1977.

7.

CONFERENCE REFLECTIONS

Roger Frank Swanson

It is now almost commonplace to observe that one of the para-
doxes of our time is the fact that the world is fragmenting
and globalizing at the same time. As centripetal forces bring
the world closer together in the economic sphere, centrifugal
forces are thrusting the world farther apart as national and
subnational groups seek to define and further their distinctiveness. A major component of this drive for distinctiveness
is the phenomenon of cultural nationalism. In the most basic
sense, "Independent statehood does not by itself provide the
means of maintaining all the separateness that people want to
maintain."[1] One need look no further than Canada to see this
phenomenon in action.

All nations in the international community are in varying
degrees concerned with independence and separateness, but the
Canadian concern is in a sense unique. Unanimous in their
opinion that survival was, and is, the main theme of the Canadian national experience, the questions Canadians could not
agree upon were: survival of what, and against whom? What
was this emerging entity called Canada? Was it an artificial
political construct superimposed on the North American continent in defiance of geography and economics, or was it geo-
graphically and economically a national community? And where
was one to look for Canada's cultural roots: in its "Europeanness"? -- or in its "North Americanness"? -- or in a new
synthesis of "Canadianness"? An equally compelling question
was: Against whom were Canadians trying to survive? Was it
the British, the United States, or internal divisiveness between English-speaking and French-speaking Canada? The search
for answers to these questions goes to the heart of Canada's
historical and cultural development and to the heart of the
current Canadian quest for a national identity as a sovereign
distinct nation.

It is difficult for many Americans to appreciate fully that the Canadian drama of national survival has not definitively played itself out. Canada of course developed from a colony to a nation through the achievement of responsible government and an autonomous international status. However, two ingredients of the Canadian concern for survival remain active. Internally, Canada continues its attempt to achieve political and cultural accommodation between English- and French-speaking Canada, coupled with attempts to reduce regional economic disparity. Externally, the Canadian concern about national survival involves a continued and revitalized resistance to U.S. economic and cultural influences in a Canadian attempt to maintain separateness on the North American continent.

It is also difficult for many Americans to appreciate the relative uniqueness of the cultural interaction between Canada and the United States. There is, of course, a certain universality about the U.S. cultural impact on other nations in the international community, an impact that is not everywhere welcomed. While it is helpful to place the Canadian concern about the U.S. cultural impact in a global setting, sight must not be lost of two factors which make the Canada-U.S. case rather special. First, there is the factor of "technical accessibility."[2] Quite simply, the mechanics of cultural transmission (television, for example) make the immense and vigorous U.S. cultural base readily available to Canadians at relatively low cost. But the technical ability to transmit culture (that is, export it, or import it, depending upon the viewpoint of the observer) is not enough. There must also be a host receptivity to this U.S. cultural base, which brings us to the second factor. Because of certain cultural similarities between the United States and English-speaking Canada, and because of a genuine overall Canadian responsiveness (which often includes French Canadians) to various forms of U.S. culture, the U.S. cultural message finds a largely receptive if not universally eager audience in Canada.

But where does one go from here? Canadians are concerned about national survival in the face of the U.S. cultural impact; this impact is exacerbated by the easy mechanics of cultural transmission; and Canadians are genuinely receptive to U.S. cultural forms. Thus began the fourth Lester B. Pearson Conference on the Canada-U.S. Relationship. To this U.S. participant, the discussions were comprehensive, articulate, and provocative. No transborder consensus emerged from the conference, nor was there any attempt to homogenize sometimes sharply divergent positions. In short, while the discussions were inconclusive, they were useful in identifying the host of elements that simply must be considered in assessing Canada-U.S. cultural issues.

But perhaps even more important and revealing than the issues discussed were the actual dynamics of the discussions. In a microcosm, the conference captured the sincere goodwill that exists between Canadians and Americans and the difficulties in translating this goodwill into concrete policy suggestions that might help neutralize the irritants confronting the Canada-U.S. relationship in the cultural sector. It is at this point that the question -- where does one go from here? -- tends to become circular in nature. That is, conference discussions of the cultural issues in a general sense seemed to move through four phases, albeit in a rather erratic manner coming full circle by the end of the conference.

Discussions began with the "explanatory phase," whereby the Canadian guests explained to the Americans the underlying reasons for their cultural concerns and the need for specific Canadian policies. In turn, the American guests expressed their concern about these policies. Americans are ready listeners, if difficult to convince, and so the discussion went, occasionally tripping over such words as "anti-American" and "nationalism." Discussions soon moved to the "agreement-in-principle phase." Although unconvinced about the intrinsic wisdom of specific Canadian policies, some of which made Americans shudder in that these policies seemed contrary to their vision of the free flow of information, the discussions moved to higher and higher levels of generality. For the Americans, this phase culminated in the assertion that they were obviously not challenging the right of Canadians to do that which they think necessary to preserve the Canadian nation.

Discussions then moved to the third stage, which is the "technique phase." By now there was disagreement about specific policies, but broad agreement in principle about the respective sovereign powers of the two nations. Those Americans who conceded the Canadian power to set policies which are disadvantageous to U.S. interests addressed themselves instead to the Canadian technique of implementing their policies. For example, while strongly disagreeing with the Canadian policies toward _Time_ magazine, several American participants expressed concern about the Canadian implementation of its policy rather than about the need for or wisdom of the policy. The discussions then moved into the fourth stage, the "search for bilateral solutions phase." Suggestions abounded as to the means of solving some of the Canada-U.S. cultural issues, including a suggested cultural "free trade" area as in the Auto Pact, a special clause under GATT, and the possibility of a bilateral organization responsible for cultural matters.

Bilateral solutions are hard to come by, however, and the discussion tended to come full circle by reverting to the "explanatory phase" wherein Canadians again explained to their American counterparts the reasons for and wisdom of their cultural concerns and policies. The conference culminated with movement to the "agreement-in-principle phase," in which Americans assured Canadians that the cultural problems involved implementative techniques rather than any basic disagreement on fundamentals.

This circular characterization of the conference dynamics obviously oversimplifies extremely complicated issues and a highly sophisticated discussion of these issues. At the same time, one cannot help but notice the self-closing circular quality of the discussions and conclude that there are fundamental definitional questions that remain unanswered. Indeed, the case can be made that the basic problem facing the Canada-U.S. relationship is really definitional in nature. In the broadest sense, the question is: What sort of relationship do we want, and what are our respective rights and obligations as Canadian and American actors in this relationship? It was this question with which the conference participants so eloquently wrestled.

But an even more basic question inheres in this broad question and, in fact, is a prerequisite to answering the broader question. When should we "bilateralize"? On the abstract level, to what extent should we jointly define the sort of relationship that we want, or should this be done individually? And on the policy level, are the problems confronting the relationship, in this case the cultural sector, amenable to bilateral solutions, or must the answer be found first on the unilateral level? Can it be that in an international system plagued by ungentle adversaries, the Canada-U.S. relationship is burdened by too much togetherness? The case can be made that Americans and Canadians try to decide things together before we have decided things separately using national rather than bilateral criteria.

In the Canada-U.S. cultural relationship, we are confronted with a Canada that desires to be more distinctly differentiated from the United States. This involves change, which in turn involves redefinition and adjustment. But first, this redefinition must take place on a unilateral rather than bilateral basis. Assessments and reassessments must first take place in the respective capitals of Ottawa and Washington, not at a negotiating table. Rather than a search for techniques to resolve bilateral issues, there should first be a unilateral search in Ottawa and Washington for internal decision-making procedures that will ensure an effective cost/benefit assessment of the policies of differentiation and of the impact of these policies on the other nation. It is at this point that consultation and negotiation become the essential ingredients of a successful bilateral relationship whereby officials of the other government are alerted to the impact of changing policies on their interests.

It is almost a form of heresy in the traditional Canada-U.S. dialogue to point out that "good" bilateral relations are not necessarily the ultimate goal of both nations. Instead, the goal involves the attempted realization of our respective national interests, and the implementation of these interests can involve high costs when they diverge as they now seem to be doing. This is not to suggest "bad" relations as a tonic for the relationship, and it would, of course, be foolish to underestimate the need for cooperative bilateral techniques, especially during a time of rapid change. However, the search for bilateral techniques must not become an end in itself or a substitute for inadequate decision-making procedures and cost/benefit assessments in Ottawa and Washington. This does not mean repudiating those bilateral techniques that have proved so successful, such as the International Joint Commission. Rather, it is a call for greater attention to internal procedures, coupled with a more realistic assessment of the limited bilateral solutions available, given the changing continental and international milieus. Certainly, it is misleading to assume in the mid-1970s that Canadian and U.S. policies are not significantly divergent and that our problems are primarily a function of inadequate bilateral consultative techniques rather than basic policy differences and procedures.

If only Canadians were more systematic in developing consistent long-range policies, says the U.S. observer. Ah, but if only Americans were more flexible and patient in acknowledging domestic Canadian requisites, the Canadian observer notes. Translated, this simply means that if we were more like each other, we would have fewer problems, a dubitable proposition at best. For Americans, it is rather like looking in a mirror. We are sincerely fond of, and satisfied with, the image. But should that image take on a life of its own, independent of our norms and preferences, I suspect that we would become confused if not disoriented. Attempts to adjust to this disorientation are in the first case a unilateral problem. Certainly, it is doubtful whether the creation of a joint committee would be particularly useful in reconciling a schizophrenic condition.

Canadians and Americans learned to live with their similarities during the intimate postwar period, but can we now learn to live with our differences? If this conference is any indication, the answer is entirely in the affirmative, although there will be significant difficulties and adjustments. Such are my random reflections. If they are rather abstract in nature, it is because I had the impression during the conference that we were dealing with far more intangible and fundamental issues than Time magazine and deletion of U.S. commercials from American programs carried on Canadian cable television.

My paper, "Canadian Cultural Nationalism and the U.S. Public Interest," attempted to answer a basic question -- when should we bilateralize -- from a U.S. perspective. Although there were extremely useful insights garnered from other conference participants, my views on major points were not materially altered. It is interesting, and significant, that no one challenged my premise that Canadian cultural nationalism is a legitimate area of concern on the part of the U.S. government. However, many participants wondered with some degree of amazement how some of these cultural issues (commercial deletion, for example) could be given such a high priority by the U.S. government in view of the other pressing matters on its international agenda. But here again, the second premise of my paper was that U.S. policy toward Canada is the outcome of a highly complex and dynamic bargaining process in Washington.

If I had to summarize the overall Canadian position at the conference, a hazardous task at best given the diversity of opinions, I would do so with the following sentence: "The risks latent in the Americanization of Canada may easily be overstated at the moment, but they must not be ignored, and no means of lessening them should be missed."3 It is relevant to note that this sentence did not emanate from the conference; it was written in 1903. This suggests that the conference was dealing with a phenomenon that is enduring as well as confusing.

And so these reflections have come full circle, as did the conference discussions. Canadians are concerned about national survival in face of the U.S. cultural impact; this impact is furthered by the easy mechanics of cultural transmission; and Canadians are genuinely receptive to U.S. cultural forms. The conference message, to me at least, was that the contradictions of interdependence and separateness are in the first instance national rather than bilateral problems. Americans cannot reconcile the Canadian ambivalence over these contradictions, nor can Canadians develop a sense of proportion and patience for Americans. Once we have nationally assessed what type of relationship we want, and developed adequate decision-making procedures and cost/benefit assessments in our respective capitals, we can address ourselves to those transborder techniques of issue resolution that would allow both nations to realize their goals with a minimum of bilateral disturbance. In the meanwhile, as I concluded in my paper, it is essential that both Canadians and Americans develop a more sophisticated awareness of the governmental and private forces active in each other's country.

February 1977

NOTES

1. Harold R. Isaacs, "Nationality: 'End of the Road'?" Foreign Affairs, Vol. 53, No. 3 (April 1975), p. 445. See also Arnfinn Jorgensen-Dahl, "Forces of Fragmentation in the International System: The Case of Ethno-Nationalism," Orbis, Vol. XIX, No. 2 (Summer 1975), pp. 652-74.

2. See Andrew M. Scott, The Revolution in Statecraft (New York: Random House, 1969).

3. As quoted in "The Progress of Events: The U.S. and Canada," Current Literature (Current Opinion), Vol. XXXIV (April 1903), p. 386. The quotation is from an article in the London Monthly Review.

8.

PEARSON IV: A CANADIAN IMPRESSION

Michael Barkway

Throughout the discussions on "cultural nationalism," it
seemed to me, we teetered on the thin edge between philosophy and politics, between principles and procedures. As
anyone might have foreseen, good old American pragmatism
triumphed. The temptation to view current preoccupations
in a wider and longer context was presented more than once;
fascinating vistas were glimpsed at the bottom of the gar-
den, but our eyes dutifully returned to the green-baize-
covered table.

This was almost foreordained by the nature of the
subject -- or, rather, by the avoidance of any attempt
to define what we meant by culture. The case-study
method left us with Time magazine, TV commercials, films,
book publishing, and the nationality of university professors; and these in turn raised two questions to which
the discussion returned, in one form or another, again
and again:

  -- To what extent were these "cultural" questions proper
     matters of concern to governments? And
  -- Should they, when so regarded, be treated as economic
     matters; or did they call for new apparatus (differ-
     ent "channels," specialized commissions, or new
     "joint" bodies)?

The discussion did not start on this level, and various participants (mainly from the U.S. side) repeatedly
interjected questions and observations of more fundamental
significance. The wider context helps, I think, to put the
more practical, procedural, and political questions in perspective.

The Historical Context

We were reminded at our first session how much change had taken place since the first Pearson conference met five years ago in 1971. The agenda prepared for that meeting by John Dickey and John Holmes covered a range of subjects, starting with "What should the two countries want: bilaterally, multilaterally"? It included a section on "problem-solving" between Canada and the United States, asking whether there was any prospect of "building toward a more developed concept through functional cooperation." "No one," it was said, "would write that agenda today." But it was a reminder how crucial to Canada-U.S. relations is a sense of history.

Since 1971, said one close American observer, Canadian nationalism had seemed again and again to have peaked. But it never did. What did happen was that it was translated from preaching into practice. In terms both of history and of nationalism-in-action, this five-year perspective could well be stretched to the last thirty years since World War II; and there were several serious predictions from Canadian participants (notably those in official positions) that government intervention in cultural affairs must be expected to grow over the next decade or so. More "confrontations" were regarded as inevitable.

It is instructive to recall the wave of concern about Canadian nationalism which arose in 1957-58, after the Diefenbaker government came into power. In 1958, I wrote a piece entitled "Canada Rediscovers Its History," which I concluded by saying:

> The restoration of a proper historical balance in Canada's outlook will restore the essential tension of Canada's equivocal position between the two worlds of history and geography. It will make for more realistic judgments of American policy. It should restore the kind of relationship which is normal and proper between neighbors, in which a few hard words now and then keep things on a realistic basis.[1]

Several American comments at the conference suggested that this happy result is at least a bit nearer achievement. I noted, for example, one statement that the United States had shown more restraint over some recent Canadian actions than would have been considered possible a few years ago. The "rediscovery of history" (still largely unconscious) in

Canada was a long time coming. It followed "the great aberration" of the Mackenzie King era when (as the historian Donald Creighton said) the Liberals found it politically profitable to pose as defenders of Canadian independence against British dominance long after it had ceased to be any threat. Political convenience obstructs rational policy in Canada as well as in the United States. It was, amongst other things, the reason why the controversy over the Canadian edition of _Time_ was prolonged over twenty years instead of being finished in 1956; and it is still the only discernible reason for the exemption of _Reader's Digest_ in 1976.

What Is Distinctive About Canadian Culture?

Mainly its history -- British traditions of constitutional government; and hitherto an attempt to embrace within that framework the persisting language and culture of Quebec, an experiment in progress.

The most penetrating probe into this basic ground, which the conferees accepted without exploring more deeply, was made by an American participant who distinguished between the political and constitutional culture and the socio-economic. It was somewhat oversimplified in later discussion when the socio-economic tended to be equated with mass culture and the political philosophy with "high" culture. But the distinction is fundamental.

The American who introduced it contrasted the British and the American approach to the handling of power: the American distrust of it, with the resulting emphasis on checks and balances, and the British concentration on ways of harnessing it and using it. In this political culture, Canada and the United States were different. But the speaker doubted whether any political approach could make much difference to the socio-economic culture in either country. If Canadian governments could shut out all American influences, they still could not shape the socio-economic culture which was developing in all post-industrial societies. Nobody, in the United States or Canada or anywhere else, could shape or control that.

This was accepted by the Canadian who responded. Popular or mass culture was moving on similar lines in all the post-industrial societies. The differences came at the margin, but they were still important. Instead of McLuhan's "global village," there was an upsurge of increasing local nationalisms all over the world. In Canada it appeared as a strong reassertion of regional feeling. Quebec was the obvious case, but regionalism was rampant everywhere. (To be fair to McLuhan -- who, after all, makes a virtue of discontinuities rather than coherence -- he also proclaims the phenomenon of "retribalization" with a corresponding increase in violence.) This relates to the disparities of scale which (the Canadians insisted) are a vital element in Canada's cultural nationalism, as in nearly all Canada-U.S. problems.

In the heyday of American technocracy and "scientific management" (so-called), Jacques Servan-Schreiber wrote a book urging that Europe's salvation lay in emulating these American skills; and Canada was almost equally impressed. But the technocratic gospel has lost much of its magic in the 1970s, and McLuhan quips: "Europe is the place where old American ideas go when they die."

The turmoil of post-industrial culture is marked, amongst other things, by a general revolt against "bigness" -- whether in government, business and labour, or in the "Ed. Biz." and even the medical establishment (see Ivan Illich's recent book, Limits to Medicine). J. B. Priestley coined the term "Admass" before Ralph Nader was loved by anyone but his mother; and Admass dominates popular culture in nearly all "advanced" countries. But it is also true that, especially in English-speaking countries, Admass is dominated by American influences and often by American money. Inevitably, that is particularly true of English-speaking Canada, and we were told that it is increasingly true of Quebec through dubbed movies and TV shows. The sheer weight of this American mass culture was described by Canadian conferees in every field -- broadcasting, films, periodicals, books, and even university campuses. Hence the much-discussed question whether cultural affairs could be separated from economic questions, at least in inter-government discussions.

Culture vs. Economics

As a matter of current fact, American participants said that any Canadian cultural actions which came under the notice of the U.S. government were handled through the channels which handle economic questions. Indeed, the reason for government involvement at all was usually the fact that American private interests were affected.

In the cases causing concern this year, the most sensitive was Canadian legislation applying to border TV stations the same principle already applied to Canadian advertising in print media: Advertising expenditures by Canadians on U.S. media for advertisements addressed to Canadians will no longer be tax deductible. The subject matter of this legislation has never been open to negotiation with the U.S. government, but it has aroused threats of retaliatory action by the Congress. All the American participants warned that this threat must be taken seriously. Knowledgeable Canadians said it already had been.

Other sore points included a regulation by the Canadian Radio-Television Commission providing for deletion of commercial messages from U.S. TV programmes carried on Canadian cable systems (which is open for discussion with Washington), and the extension of the rule about advertising expenditures in "non-Canadian periodicals" to the Canadian edition of Time while Reader's Digest of Canada still gets exemption, though on fairly stringent conditions. There appeared to be pretty general agreement by Canadian and American participants that these last two cases, at least, had been very badly handled. As one Canadian said of Time, "it was very badly handled, but it had to be done." Furthermore, Canadians concerned with the media (in government as well as business) agreed that we were only at the beginning of the road.

Approaches were now being made to see if it was possible to arrange for wider showing of Canadian films in foreign-owned theatre chains by agreement with the owners. Such agreements might be a test of what could be achieved by negotiation with private interests without resorting to legislation or government compulsion. Other fields under study were book publishing and newsstand distribution.

All the Canadian suggestions for government involvement aroused two deeply rooted fears, expressed by several American participants:
1. "The First Amendment Optic," as it was called. One Canadian swept it aside in a fine burst of indignation. "Really," he said in effect, "Canadians don't need to be lectured about freedom of speech!" Other Canadians, without disagreeing, recognized that it was a delicate task to regulate channels of communication without interfering; but, delicate or not, they said the government must and would go on trying to open up more channels for Canadian products.
2. "The Pure Canada Cult," as it was called long ago by John Farthing in his book Freedom Wears a Crown (1952), put together by the late Judith Robinson. Farthing effectively mocked nationalists who dreamed of "a Canadian culture springing spontaneously from the barren rocks of the Laurentian Shield."

That the cult is not quite dead is shown in Miss Crean's book Who's Afraid of Canadian Culture?, but participants in this conference were satisfied that the cultists have been reduced to a small minority in English-speaking Canada.

The growth of more moderate nationalism was attributed, at least in part, to the fact that government had been prodded into more active support for Canadian cultural products. (In Quebec, nearly all participants told the opposite story.) The problem, as Canadian participants put it, was not the risk of insulating English Canada from international influences (predominantly, but not exclusively, American): It was to make a place for even a modest proportion of Canadian content in the media.

In one important respect, the "economic" or "market" approach to cultural matters was matched by the official Canadian attitude on such matters as the Canadian edition of Time and advertising on border stations addressed to Canadians. "The aim," said one Canadian, "is to maximize the advertising revenues available in Canada for spending on Canadian productions." The same was true of revenues derived from sale and distribution of films, books, and periodicals. As the ad men say, "money is the name of the game." The unstated conclusion seemed to match the view expressed by sociologists like Daniel Bell -- that the balance of private and public interests cannot be left to market forces.[2]

Canadian speakers accepted American warnings that actions designed to increase the amount of money available for Canadian content in the media by reducing the amount taken out of Canada by American entrepreneurs would run into opposition and possible retaliation. Private American interests which were hurt would have a political impact. "These private-interest cases," said one American, "are highly explosive." It was on this ground that Americans repeatedly emphasized the importance of the manner, or "style," adopted by the Canadian government.

Quebec

Whatever the difficulties presented by the cultural nationalism of English-speaking Canada, the problem in French-speaking Quebec was described in terms which were both sharper and more gloomy.

In the absence of French-speaking Québécois living in the province, the conference depended on Canadians (of both mother tongues) and Americans who are in close touch with Quebec without being "of" it. All expressed anxiety about growing isolation, cultural as well as political.

French Canadians, they agreed, were less "hung up" on fear of American dominance than their fellow citizens of the English language: It was frequently stated that they felt American influences less directly from the United States than from indirect transmission through Toronto. For French Canada, said one, language and culture are the same word. Without firm assurance of the preservation of the language, "then only fear will postpone separation for Quebec."

A Canadian historian, closely concerned with Quebec, underlined the point, saying, "Quebec's culture is very weak. All that's left is the language." He mentioned the astonishingly rapid decline in the influence of the Roman Catholic church and the general adoption of birth control (no more "revanche du berceau").

"High" culture in Quebec, it was said, was the concern of a very small élite (as, indeed, it is everywhere), and this élite was increasingly inward-looking and isolationist. The "mass" culture, on the other hand, was more exposed than ever to American "Admass" through films, television, and advertising with dubbed French speech. It was even questioned whether, if most Québécois became bilingual, the majority would wish to emigrate to greener anglophone pastures.

One sideline, which only seemed to emphasize the pessimistic tone of the discussions about Quebec, was a question addressed to the Americans about their attitude to a possible separation. We were told that some Québécois were speculating that American sympathies might be aroused if their assertion of independence from Canada were accompanied by violence. Emphatically No, said an American. There would be no doubt in Washington, he asserted, that a united Canada serves the best interests of the United States.

With that limited degree of comfort the Canadians were left to contemplate their chances of establishing "a more perfect union."

October 1976

- 134 -

1. Michael Barkway, "Canada Rediscovers Its History,"
    Foreign Affairs, Vol. 36, No. 3 (April 1958), p. 417.

2. See Daniel Bell, The Cultural Contradictions of
    Capitalism (New York: Basic Books, 1976), e.g., "The
    consumer-oriented, free-enterprise society no longer
    morally satisfies the citizenry, as it once did. A
    new public philosophy will have to be created . . ."
    (p. 251); or, "The market . . . has to be seen as a
    mechanism, not a principle of justice" (p. 277).

9.

A WORD OF PERSONAL PERSPECTIVE

John Sloan Dickey

As one of the "founding participants" of the Lester B.
Pearson Conferences, the significance of the fourth conference was highlighted for me by the fact that the discussions focused on what I regard as the two foremost con-
tinuities of concern in the affairs of today's relationship
between Canada and the United States: the management of
nationalism and the development of better processes for
fashioning both policy and understanding.

In today's U.S.-Canada relationship, use of the term
"nationalism" ranges from the garden-variety "national interest" that underlies most national policies to extreme pejorative charges of "imperialism" (American) or "anti-American"
xenophobia (Canadian). Neither of these extreme views has
received much attention in the four conferences, but the
agenda of Pearson IV brought front and center the need to
face squarely the growing concern in Canada, especially as it
has been recently manifested in governmental policies, that
the American presence, particularly in the broad reach of
cultural affairs, may pose a threat to the well-being of
Canada's independent nationhood. Cultural nationalism as the
central subject of Pearson IV also assured frank instructive
discussion of another threat to Canadian nationhood which had
received little attention in the previous conferences, namely,
the growing schism between Quebec and the rest of Canada.
Here, as events were shortly to confirm, the participants
were discussing an ancient cultural nationalism whose defense
and assertion portended a crisis of fathomless consequence
for Canada.

The subject of nationalism in one form or another was
inevitably touched on in each of the preceding conferences.
The first conference in 1971, for example, while not expli-

citly emphasizing nationalism as a growing factor in the affairs of the relationship, left little doubt that a significant weather change had already begun in the way the two countries conceived their relationship to each other. In particular, the early rhetoric of "partnership," "special relationship," "integration," "North American system," etc., no longer accorded with mounting Canadian nationalistic concern that dependence on things American had reached dangerous levels.

Throughout the subsequent conferences on energy and business-labor relations, there was a growing recognition within both participant groups that the most basic continuity of concern within the contemporary relationship for both nations must be the rational management and, where appropriate, the restraint of their respective nationalisms, and especially the avoidance of resort to retaliatory responses of beggar-thy-neighbor.

It was not, however, until five years later that the planners of the agenda for Pearson IV decided that the time had come when the purpose of the conferences could, indeed must, move head-on into the emotional heartland of nationalistic controversy -- cultural nationalism. As the preceding papers and summary of the conference make clear, the mass media aspect of the subject, involving at once national sensibilities, powerful private interests, and the technological outreach of modern communication, is about as bifurcated in respect to the forces of the past and the future as international affairs get.

Understanding another society's nationalism in a truly profound sense is an unlikely achievement even for disinterested scholars, but it is an especially difficult assignment for professionals and laymen alike when adversary considerations must also be weighed and met; and this was inescapably the case in Pearson IV with the three disparate nationalisms of Canada, French Canada, and the United States. While stopping short of seeming wise with the benefit of the rerun of the conference in the foregoing pages, I doubt that anything other than a multidimensional process such as that of the Pearson conferences could have produced the perspectives of depth, breadth, and examined self-interest that made Pearson IV a genuine achievement as an approach to shared understanding.

Moreover, beyond the substantive perspectives that may have been improved by Pearson IV, the tangled interests of cultural nationalism apparently aroused more consideration of possibilities for better processes in the official affairs of the relationship. At the closing session of the conference, several people who have made the Canada–U.S. relationship part of their professional life, in addition to praising the processes of the conference, volunteered a guarded hope. Despite their inbred skepticism about the general value of efforts to deal with substantive problems of international affairs through added organizational structure and codified principles, perhaps, just perhaps, the management of the future of electronic communication between the two societies might profit from more creative attention to the development of functionally defined joint agencies for more effective oversight and more timely attention of such matters. In this as in their substantive exchanges, the outcome of these conferences undoubtedly is down the road a ways, but it will probably be just such ongoing learning in the processes of understanding that gives their mixed private-"official" perspective the possibility of being notable.

Beyond the difficult but never-ending task of statecraft to keep the official processes of the bilateral relationship effectively attuned to the developing transnational interests of the two governments, there is the underlying need in the U.S.-Canada relationship, probably as in no other, to attend the processes that nurture the quality of citizen understanding that must undergird its well-nigh unlimited private-public interplay. It was this overarching consideration that led the Council on Foreign Relations and the Canadian Institute of International Affairs to sponsor these joint conferences aimed at developing processes calculated to further a more profound, shared understanding on the part of public and private persons in both countries. Negotiations, decisions, agreements, and solutions are to be left to other processes, other forums.

The process whereby such shared understanding is sought in the Pearson conferences has now been tested in such varied fields as the conceptual framework of the relationship, energy problems, North American security arrangements, multinational business and union activities, and the emotionally charged issues of cultural nationalism. A definitive evaluation of the conferences is not in order here, but this participant can testify that the multidimensioned process of Pearson IV, involving perspectives of history, diverse regions, national and private interests, politics, seasoned professionals as well as newcomers uninhibited by either the emperor's raiment or lack of it, over four days of give-and-

take, with no score kept, produced an impressive binational
willingness to seek greater shared understanding. Such a
willingness is no small achievement.

February 1977